Table of Contents

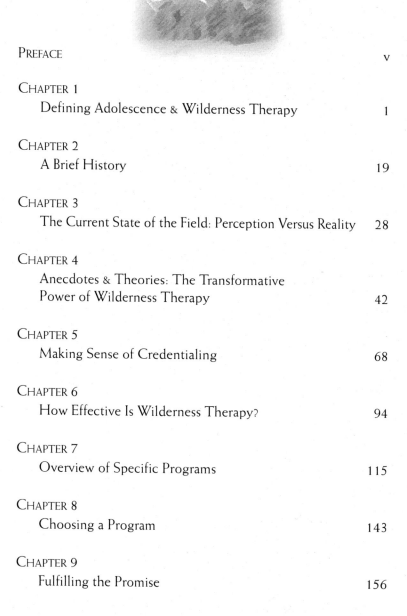

Preface

In 1994, we published a book, *Wilderness Therapy: Foundations, Theory and Research* (Davis-Berman & Berman, 1994), that served as the first book in what was, at the time, a relatively new field. Our target audience for that book was therapists and outdoor leaders working with adolescents.

Our interest and involvement in the field started in 1985, when Dene was the administrator of a psychiatric hospital, where many of the patients remained on a locked inpatient unit for months at a time, only going outside for brief periods on the grounds of the hospital. Watching how adolescents reacted to those brief forays outside led him to contemplate the potential therapeutic effects of taking the adolescents into the wilderness as an alternative or a complement to staying on a locked inpatient unit. A review of the extant literature on the topic revealed little empirical data. Jen, having recently completed her graduate education in social work, jumped in as issues of program design and data collection emerged. These efforts led, in the late 1980s, to the publication of some of the earliest research studies on the effects of wilderness therapy (Berman & Davis-Berman, 1989; Davis-Berman & Berman, 1989).

In 1986, Jen became a professor at the University of Dayton. At about the same time Dene left the hospital, and together we started a private counseling practice called Lifespan Counseling Associates. From its inception, our practice included the Wilderness Therapy Program. We developed wilderness therapy trips for adolescents who were in the juvenile court system, for others who were abused or neglected and were living in Children's Services homes, and for others who were in outpatient counseling and in need of a more intensive therapy experience. Dependent on the type of trip and the population, these wilderness therapy trips ranged from a few days to a few weeks in length.

These days, we no longer lead wilderness therapy trips but instead refer clients to organizations that specialize in such programming. The reasons for this reflect numerous trends in the field that are covered in this book. First, there is an increasing awareness of the legal difficulties in taking adolescents across state lines and practicing counseling in other states. Second, while insurance companies used to have lenient policies about the variety of mental health services they would cover, now there are just too many hoops to jump through to secure payment for services. And third, dealing with the regulations, insurance companies, liability issues, etc., requires an infrastructure that is beyond the scope of our private practice. Instead, our interests have evolved into teaching leadership skills, especially those that interface with the field of counseling, to outdoor educators, while we continue to write and speak on issues related to psychotherapy and the wilderness.

The impetus for our first book was a deep concern about adolescent mental health issues and the need for more innovative treatment programs to address the challenges that young people face. Today, the pressures and stressors facing adolescents have only increased. As a result, parents and families need information and support more than ever. It is for this reason that this new book is written with parents in mind, so that they may find answers and information that will help guide them through the process of making decisions about treatment for their teenagers. Hopefully, this book can also serve as a resource for mental health and outdoor professionals unfamiliar with wilderness therapy as a treatment approach, as we all are working toward a similar goal: To try to improve the health and well-being of our clients.

We have titled this book *The Promise of Wilderness Therapy* with the intent of using the word *promise* in two ways. Promise, as used in this title, reflects both the potential that this approach has for helping people, as well as the promises that practitioners make to clients, either implicitly or explicitly, about the efficacy and safety of this approach. Topics we address concern the extent to which wilderness therapy lives up to its promise as a treatment and the extent to which wilderness therapy programs deliver on the promises they make when offering their services.

As a treatment approach, wilderness therapy primarily serves adolescents. Thus, the focus of this book is on this age group. That is why we start the book with a brief view of some of the stressors facing adolescents today. This is not to say that wilderness therapy does not or cannot have effective applications for other populations, only that we have chosen to address the primary population served by wilderness therapy.

In the past decade, many wilderness therapy programs have forayed into the formal arena of psychiatric care. In so doing, they have entered the behavioral health care field, which provides "mental health and substance abuse/dependence care services" (McKenzie, Ringer, & Kotecki, 2005). While there are also a host of programs that use the wilderness to help people as an adjunct to traditional therapy or in lieu of therapy, we will not be focusing on those programs in this book. Our emphasis will be on those programs that provide professional behavioral health care services to troubled youth. This is because we view wilderness therapy as a behavioral health care service.

There are those who do not agree with our definition of what constitutes a wilderness therapy program and best practices for the field. Throughout this book, we strive to make clear when and how our opinions have influenced the information we provide. Furthermore, even though we are involved with the international wilderness therapy community (Berman & Davis-Berman, 2006), as North Americans practicing in the state of Ohio, we know that our perspectives on certification and professionalization are not universally shared. For example, our discussions on insurance coverage for wilderness therapy will not resonate with our colleagues in countries with national health care. In an effort to shed some light on what is going on internationally, Chapter 5 (the section on this book that addresses credentialing) includes information about credentialing initiatives in various parts of the world.

When we approached AEE about publication of this book, we were enthusiastically encouraged to do so by Kris Von Wald, Ph.D., the executive director of AEE at the time. Thanks, Kris, for sharing our vision and encouraging us to embark on this journey. To Natalie Kurylko, AEE's director of publications, thank you for helping us take our vision and turn it into a manuscript of which we can be proud. You have worked tirelessly on this project, and your dedication and professionalism are much appreciated and admired.

Two people have served as reviewers of our manuscript: Steven Beyer, Ph.D., J.D., and Simon Crisp, Ph.D. Their comments have been invaluable. From them, we have broadened our perspectives, reconceptualized some of our beliefs, and honed our language. Steve and Simon, we appreciate your wisdom and appreciate your willingness to serve as sounding boards.

Many individuals have contributed to this book in more informal ways. Two friends have helped shape our own thoughts about wilderness therapy through the years: David Thobaben and Mark Gillen, Ph.D. To Will White, M.S.W., who reviewed the manuscript with a particular eye to programs and credentialing, thank you. Thanks to Keith Russell, Ph.D., for his feedback on research and information on OBHIC. Thank you also to Michael Gass, Ph.D., for his feedback on Chapters 3 and 5. To Colin Goldthorpe, who runs a model wilderness therapy program in New Zealand, thanks for your insights and encouragement. We have appreciated the many conversations about the nature of therapy over the years with Denise Mitten, the founder of Woodswomen. Pete Allison has been most helpful in providing information about credentialing in Great Britain. To the many people who have given us feedback about our first book and ideas that have percolated since then at conferences, in response to articles, and during WEA courses in the field, we also express our gratitude.

References

Berman, D., & Davis-Berman, J. (1989). Wilderness therapy: A therapeutic adventure for adolescents. *Journal of Independent Social Work* 3(3), 65–77.

Berman, D., & Davis-Berman, J. (2006, February). The promise of wilderness therapy. Keynote address presented at the 4th International Adventure Therapy Conference, Rotorua, New Zealand.

Davis-Berman, J., & Berman, D. (1989). The Wilderness Therapy Program: An empirical study of its effects with adolescents in an outpatient setting. *Journal of Contemporary Psychotherapy* 19(4), 271–281

Davis-Berman, J., & Berman, D. (1994). *Wilderness therapy: Foundations, theory and research.* Dubuque, IA: Kendall/Hunt.

McKenzie, J., Ringer, R., & Kotecki, J. (2005). *An introduction to community health* (5th Ed.). Sudbury, MA: Jones and Bartlett.

CHAPTER 1

Defining Adolescense & Wilderness Therapy

There is no single type of adolescent to whom wilderness therapy is best suited. It is a treatment approach that can be used to help many types of individuals address some of their problems and family issues, as well as a variety of the challenges that face adolescents today. But, like other forms of psychological counseling, wilderness therapy is not a panacea for all struggling adolescents. It does, however, hold out promise for many youth.

By way of introduction, consider the following three vignettes, which illustrate the types of personal and family issues that may be effectively addressed with wilderness therapy.

Danny is a 16-year-old boy who has struggled with both depression and anxiety. He has never been sure of the source of his pain, but life has always seemed difficult for him. He comes from an intact family who, on the surface, seem very supportive. Danny denies drug or alcohol use and his parents have never seen any evidence of use. Danny is fairly sullen, doesn't talk much and spends lots of time at home alone in his room. Danny is a marginal student in school and has few friends. He hasn't made much progress in outpatient counseling and is currently taking Prozac, an SSRI antidepressant medication.

Mandy is a 14-year-old girl who was taken to the emergency room due to suspected alcohol poisoning. At the hospital, she also tested positive for marijuana. Mandy's parents have a very conflictual relationship and are openly verbally abusive to each other. Both parents have a history of alcohol and drug abuse, can frequently be seen with a drink in hand, and take many prescriptions medications, including pain killers. Mandy argues a great deal with her parents and seems very resentful of their attempts to try to parent her. She spends large amounts of time with her friends and boyfriend. She continues to use alcohol and drugs and is sexually active. She has a younger brother with whom she has little relationship. Mandy is struggling with depression and at times feels suicidal.

Carl is a 17-year-old boy whose father died six months ago of cancer, after being sick for almost five years. Carl was involved in the care of his father and was with him when he died. Although they had a happy, close family, Carl's mother has recently gone on a few dates. Since his father's death, Carl has been getting in trouble by skipping school, getting in physical fights with people, and challenging his mother's authority at home. He refuses to obey curfew and, when challenged by his mother, is often verbally abusive. He has an older sister who lives in town, but is distant from the family.

Often, adolescents like Mandy, Danny, and Carl have been involved with traditional outpatient therapy. For some, a therapeutic connection was never made while, for others, the progress in therapy, which may have been good at one point, has stalled out. In such situations, wilderness therapy can be used to go beyond what has been achieved in traditional outpatient therapy. Many wilderness therapy program participants suffer from mood disorders and are being treated, with limited success, with a variety of psychiatric medications. Others are grappling with substance abuse issues. Finally, it is not unusual to have wilderness therapy participants who are experiencing difficulties with anger or impulse control. When more traditional attempts to provide assistance aren't successful, it may be appropriate to consider wilderness therapy as a treatment option.

In this first chapter, we begin by trying to shed some light on the period of adolescence by exploring some of the developmental tasks that confront teens. Then we turn to a discussion of some of the challenges and problems faced by adolescents today. The limitations of traditional counseling with adolescents are addressed, and we present an introduction to wilderness therapy. We conclude with a brief overview of the material presented in subsequent chapters.

One of the promises of wilderness therapy is that it represents an alternative approach to traditional counseling for adolescents. We are not out to convince anyone that this is the right approach for their adolescent: Rather, our aim is to provide information about some of the unique challenges of adolescence, some of the limitations of using traditional therapy with adolescents, and the promise that wilderness therapy holds. Whether this seems an appropriate modality for a particular individual is a decision that can only be made by the parents, professional, and adolescent involved.

Unique Challenges of Adolescence

Adolescence is both an exciting and tumultuous time, as young people begin to assert their independence from family and begin to strike out on their own. Erik Erikson, one of the most widely known developmental theorists, spoke and wrote extensively on the challenges of adolescence. He presented adolescence as a developmental period during which there are conflicts to be resolved that later dictate healthy functioning. If these conflicts are not successfully resolved, serious behavioral and cognitive consequences can occur in adulthood (Erikson, 1968).

Erikson asserts that there is a sequence of developmental stages through which people normally progress. He theorized that there are eight developmental phases, each characterized by interpersonal conflicts that follow biological development. If the conflict that characterizes each stage is successfully resolved, the individual is then able to move to the next stage.

Before adolescence, the individual has four major conflicts to resolve. The first, trust versus mistrust, involves the infant's ability to bond with nurturing parents during the first year of life. As a result of this contact, the child ideally comes to experience security and the beginning of a sense of identity. At approximately 18 months, a conflict regarding autonomy versus shame and doubt arises. Hopefully, autonomy prevails and the child at 4 or 5 years of age develops a sense of initiative, instead of guilt, that grows out of successful play. Finally, during the early school years, the child develops a sense of competence as the outcome of the conflict between industry versus inferiority (Erikson, 1968). (This conflict refers to the child's struggle with being active, busy, and successful in interacting in the world, versus feeling inferior, shy and unsure of him/herself.)

These first four crises reemerge in adolescence, corresponding to puberty. In order to resolve these conflicts and develop a sense of their own identity, adolescents sometimes have to create adversaries or enemies in their lives. Parents can often attest to being treated like an enemy by their teenager. The primary adolescent crisis for Erikson involves the acquisition of a sense of identity versus confusion. Typifying this period is role experimentation. Adolescents must develop a sense of bodily identity, not an easy task given the radical changes taking place at the time of puberty. Then, social roles are explored, often in relation to the roles modeled by parents and others. When these conflicts are successfully resolved, the adolescent hopefully comes away with a sense of self (derived from healthy relationships) and convictions about a positive set of values (Erikson, 1968).

Unfortunately, such an outcome is not always achieved. When a sense of identity is not attained, the adolescent may become confused and feel lost, with little sense of family or community relationships to foster individuation and separation. Another unhealthy pattern involves negative identity (Erikson, 1968). In this case, adolescents identify with things that parents, teachers, or society deem undesirable. These adolescents would prefer to be bad or dead than to be lost or controlled by parents' wishes. In sum, our experience as therapists supports Erikson's theory that adolescence involves problems and challenges, even in cases where the parents consistently have been good models. Often, family issues resolve over time. When the conflicts become too severe, however, the confusion or negativity that all adolescents experience can become pronounced or even dominant. This is often the time when families decide they need help.

Amid the struggle of a developing identity, risk-taking behaviors are prone to occur as adolescents try out new roles and responsibilities. In fact, adolescents are sometimes notorious for their risk-taking behaviors. Parents, often remembering their own risky behaviors when they were teens, are understandably worried about the behaviors of their teenagers. Of course, excessive risk-taking is cause for concern. Theorists, however, assert that some risk-taking is normal, even desirable, as adolescents attempt to establish their independence and learn how to make their own life choices (Ponton, 1997). The challenge for parents is to monitor their child's behavior closely enough to assess excessive risk, yet not be too intrusive. This is a fine line to walk given the perils that often await young people in society today.

A more complete picture of the struggles of adolescents is gained by considering the world in which they live. Changes in family structure and composition, geographic factors like inner-city dwelling, socioeconomic factors including poverty and inadequate education, and even the threat of living in a nuclear age weigh heavily on the minds of young people. Perhaps prompted by the recent violence in American schools, we have begun to pay more attention to the stress being exerted on youth in America and worldwide (Breggin, 2000). Add to this the general level of violence to which many adolescents are exposed, and one can easily see that visions of adolescence as a time of innocence, security, and little responsibility are outdated. Being an adolescent in today's world can be a pretty demanding and scary experience. Adolescence is not just a time of physical maturation and the process of adapting to this growth. Adolescents have special needs by virtue of the unique developmental issues confronting them and the problems they face in society today.

Some of the stressors that teenagers deal with are discussed by Jonathan Kozol, one of the most widely read education activists in the United States. A former teacher, Kozol is deeply concerned about children worldwide, and in the United States in particular. His work has involved examining inequities in the quality of education in the United States, exposing the impact of socioeconomic status and race on education (Kozol, 1991; 1995; 2000), and his accessible writing style eloquently portrays the plight of children and adolescents. During a recent study (Kozol, 2005), Kozol visited 60 inner-city schools largely serving minority youth. He found basic supplies and facilities lacking in these schools, leading him to question the ability of youth to lead healthy and productive lives in the midst of school deterioration. As Kozol's research reveals, the state of America's schools serves as a stressor for adolescents. His work provides a broad social context to adolescence that is critical to understanding and appreciating this experience.

Poverty is another stressor that impacts children and families worldwide. A recent report indicates that globally more than a billion children are being denied the basics of food, shelter, and other fundamental elements that they need for healthy growth and development. More than half of the children in the developing world are denied such necessities, while in 11 of 15 industrialized nations, the proportion of children in low-income families has increased over the last 10 years (UNICEF, 2005).

And, of course, even families not suffering the challenges of poverty and violence in their home or community experience strife with their adolescent. It is important to remember that for most youth and their families, adolescence is simply a time of some challenge. That said, family problems should not be minimized, as even in families with stable incomes and solid family structures, the stress of the changes of adolescence are real and can lead to other individual and family problems, such as mental health disorders.

Adolescent Mental Health: Common Disorders

Epidemiological studies try to determine how common mental health disorders are in a given population. This is often difficult because of problems with record keeping, confidentiality, and the national medical privacy standards enacted in 2003 (www.hhs.gov). It is particularly hard when trying to determine the extent of disorders in adolescents, as they are often grouped with children in research studies and reports (Brandenburg, Friedman, & Silver, 1990; Kazdin, 1989).

Another factor that makes it hard to determine the frequency of disorders is that studies use different terms and criteria for establishing the presence of a disorder. Nevertheless, estimates of mental health problems among children and youth vary from 5% to 20% of the population. The most recent report of the Surgeon General (U.S. Department of Health and Human Services, 2001) on mental health sheds some light on this issue. This report underscores the fact that often children and adolescents have disorders that fall in more than one diagnostic category. For example, an adolescent may be diagnosed with both a mood disorder and a substance abuse disorder. In fact, this is quite common because teenagers will use substances to improve their mood. Researchers estimate, however, that about 21% of children and adolescents in the United States have a diagnosable mental health disorder that is at least minimally impairing. Approximately 11% of those, or about 4 million youth have a disorder that is significantly impairing (U.S. Department of Health & Human Services, 1999; 2001).

In the United States, mental health disorders are diagnosed based on descriptions of disorders in a book called the Diagnostic and Statistical Manual, version four (DSM IV). This classification system was developed by the American Psychiatric Association and is widely used today. It uses five axes or dimensions to describe the psychological problems and functioning of individuals. Axis I reports the primary diagnosis, such as major depression or generalized anxiety disorder. Axis II reports developmental disorders (i.e., autism) and personality disorders (i.e., dissociative identity disorder). Physical conditions related to mental functioning are reported on Axis III. This includes diseases like diabetes, for example. Psychosocial stressors, like school and family problems are coded on Axis IV. Finally, Axis V involves a numerical rating of functioning (APA, 1994).

There are a number of disorders identified in the DSM IV that are usually diagnosed in infancy, childhood, or adolescence. These include: mental retardation, learning disorders, motor skills disorders, communication disorders, pervasive developmental disorders, attention deficit disorder, feeding or eating disorders, tic disorders, and elimination disorders (APA, 1994). Interestingly, these disorders are not the most commonly diagnosed in teenagers. A recent U.S. government report on mental health in adolescence found that anxiety disorders were the most common disorders, followed by conduct and mood disorders (U.S. Department of Health & Human Services, 1999; 2001). The stressors of adolescence presented earlier likely contribute to the frequency of anxiety in adolescents.

As previously stated, it is not unusual for mental health disorders and addictions to occur simultaneously. Frequently it is difficult, if not impossible, to determine which disorder occurred first. An adolescent may be depressed, for instance, and drink alcohol or use other drugs in order to feel better (referred to as self-medicating). Prolonged substance abuse, on the other hand, may itself lead to the development of mental health problems, as many substances are strong depressants and can contribute to the development of depression and anxiety. Substance abuse is a serious problem, with estimates suggesting that at least 3 million American adolescents are abusing alcohol alone (Johnson, O'Malley, & Bachman, 2003). In a study conducted in 2005, 20% of eighth graders and more than 47% of high-school seniors had consumed alcohol during the month prior to the study (Johnson et al., 2005). A recent report by the Substance Abuse and Mental Health Services Administration (SAMHSA) highlights the deleterious effects of this abuse on mental and physical health, academic performance and family life (SAMHSA, 2006).

A look at the use of psychiatric medications in this population helps reveal the scope of mental health problems in American adolescents. Estimates suggest that during the latter half of the 1990s, antidepressant drug use in the under-18 age group increased by 74% (Miller, 2000). In 2002, almost 11 million prescriptions were written for SSRI and nontricyclic antidepressants for youth under the age of 18 (Hampton, 2004). (This is a significant number considering that approximately 72 million youth were aged 18 and under in that year, and that this study only reported the use of antidepressants, not stimulants and other psychiatric medications.) Use of these antidepressant medications has decreased somewhat since the time of this report, due to the black box warnings mandated by the Food and Drug Administration (FDA) about the possible increase in suicide in children and adolescents taking SSRI antidepressant medications (Varley, 2006). For example, the number of antidepressant prescriptions written for youth aged 18 and under in the month of July 2003 was 628,227, compared with 547,405 in June of 2005 (Brown University, 2005). These figures only include antidepressants, not the mood-stabilizing or antipsychotic medications that are increasingly used to treat depression. Controversy continues about the actual role of antidepressants in increasing suicide in youth. Recent studies weigh the benefits of these medications with a possible elevation in suicide risk in young people (Vasa, Carlino, & Pine, 2006; Bridge et al., 2007).

The United States seems to "lead the world" in prescribing psychiatric medications to control the behavior of the young. Using attention deficit disorder as an example, youth in Europe and Asia are prescribed and take one tenth of the stimulants used to treat this disorder as do young people in the United States, while Canadian youth take one half as much.

Recent research done at the University of London revealed increases in the use of all psychiatric drugs among youth over the last few years in Argentina, Brazil, Canada, France, Germany, Mexico, Spain, the U.K., and the U.S. (Murray, deVries, & Wong, 2004).

Although necessary for some situations, psychiatric medication is not the sole treatment option for youth with mental health problems. Traditional psychotherapy and wilderness therapy are options that will be discussed throughout this book. Historically, children and adolescents have been notoriously underserved in the area of mental health. In the late 1980s Tuma (1989) reported that approximately 70% to 80% of U.S. children in need of mental health services were not receiving them. Unfortunately, the gap between mental health need and service hasn't narrowed in the last 15 years. In fact, estimates currently suggest that between 75% and 80% of youth who need mental health services do not receive any (U.S. Department of Health & Human Services, 1999). These statistics are still valid today. Concerns about lack of accessible treatment for depression and bipolar disorder are voiced by Raeburn (2004), while Earley (2006) writes passionately about the lack of services for chronically mentally ill youth.

Treatment Options

Presently, most mental health care for adolescents is provided in outpatient settings. The majority of these services are provided by generalists, with no special training in adolescent care, and a large proportion of these outpatient services are provided in school-based health centers (Juszczak, Melinkovich, & Kaplan, 2003). While there is no shortage of pediatricians to provide general health care to children, specialists in children's mental health treatment number far fewer. It is a mistake to assume that mental health practitioners without special training can effectively work with adolescents. At a minimum, it would seem that knowledge about adolescence and the common disorders of this time would be essential. According to the American Academy of Child and Adolescent Psychiatry, there are currently just 6,000 child psychiatrists in the United States, whereas about 15 million children and adolescents experience a diagnosable mental health problem in the course of a year. Based on these statistics, it has been estimated that at least 30,000 such psychiatrists are needed (Raeburn, 2004).

In addition to lack of appropriate service providers, place of service can also be a problem. It is often best to provide services on an outpatient basis since an adolescent can receive treatment and still live at home. In the field of mental health in general, the least restrictive environment is usually the best, and placement decisions are made with this criteria in mind. However, there are circumstances when outpatient care is not adequate, and a more restrictive environment is appropriate.

Finding a treatment facility to provide more intensive care can be difficult, because there are limited inpatient psychiatric beds for adolescents (see Table 1.1 for a description of levels of care). For example, in the United States in 1995, there were 460 private psychiatric hospitals for adolescents in operation, while in 2002 that number had decreased to 265, a reduction of 42%. The number of beds in public psychiatric hospitals has also decreased dramatically, as large public hospitals have downsized or closed. In the late 1980s the percentage of insurance reimbursements for all kinds of mental health care was about 6 percent, with the average inpatient admission for children and adolescents lasting about 40 days. This reduction is the result of the advent of managed care and the lack of reimbursement by insurance companies. Recently the reimbursement percentage has fallen to about 3%, and the average inpatient stay for an adolescent has been reduced to about 10 days (Raeburn, 2004).

Residential treatment centers can sometimes serve as an alternative to psychiatric hospitals. These facilities, like hospitals, are restrictive settings in that the adolescent is removed from the home, and some level of control is placed on the teen's ability to leave the facility. Unlike hospitals, the residential treatment centers can range from large institutions to small facilities that resemble group homes. While they are intended to serve adolescents with mental health problems, they often exclude those who are most difficult to treat, are expensive, and offer fewer mental health services than may be available in other settings, such as the inpatient facilities. Also, it is often quite difficult, and sometimes impossible, to have this level of care authorized and reimbursed by health insurance companies.

A less commonly used and more recent alternative to both inpatient and outpatient settings is partial hospitalization. As an intermediate setting, partial hospitalization involves more restrictiveness than outpatient settings but does not involve 24-hour care. Partial hospitalization can involve day treatment, sometimes at a school, where the patient receives treatment during the day and goes home at night. Some programs include full-day programming, while others have half-day programs. Clients usually participate in group education and therapy, with the option of individual sessions. Access to psychiatric services and medication management are also usually provided.

While traditional inpatient and outpatient settings or more recent combinations of the two can provide needed services to many adolescents, others are not served at all or are not served as effectively as possible by the existing services. Arriving at an appropriate solution is difficult: Although more of the traditional services are needed, with easier accessibility to them, different services are also needed.

Table 1.1 *Levels of Care*

Level of Care	Description	Pros & Cons
Outpatient	Counseling occurs in facilities in the community.	*Pro:* Least restrictive care. *Con:* Infrequent sessions. Less intense.
Intensive Outpatient	Program is based in a hospital, but clients go home at night.	*Pro:* Greater access to physicians. More intensive treatment. *Con:* Less freedom than in outpatient care.
Residential Treatment	Adolescent lives at the facility, and treatment is intensive.	*Pro:* In-depth treatment. Access to physicians and medical services. *Con:* Restrictive. Removes adolescents from their home community.
Inpatient Hospital Care	Medically oriented treatment. Usually reserved for emergency situations	*Pro:* Provides safety and stability in crisis. *Con:* Removal from home. Usually short term.

Limitations to Traditional Services

Most health insurance plans cover at least some inpatient and outpatient mental health services. While some adolescents need the structure and restrictive nature of inpatient hospital psychiatric programs, other adolescents are placed in these programs because they are in need of more intensive or restrictive services than may be available in outpatient settings. Generally, if an adolescent expresses suicidal or homicidal intent, s/he will be admitted to the hospital for a few days. One could argue that a few days in an inpatient facility is not necessarily the most effective treatment setting for a suicidal teen. Perhaps a less-restrictive environment would be more therapeutic and allow the individual to address his/her issues on a longer-term basis while remaining integrated with others. What is missing in the mental health treatment options for adolescents is a well-developed residential treatment option that is easily approved and reimbursed by health insurance.

Experience has taught us that many adolescents are hospitalized when they don't need such a restrictive setting. On one of the first wilderness therapy trips we led almost 20 years ago, we worked with adolescent inpatients from acute psychiatric hospital units. Not only did the vast majority of the clients function well in the wilderness but, in general, participant improvement during the trip was more rapid than during the hospitalized phases of their treatment (Berman & Anton, 1988).

Another limitation of inpatient services is that like many other forms of hospitalization, they encourage people to be "patients" (docile and compliant) and may even contribute to learned helplessness (Seligman, 1975). This can exacerbate whatever hopelessness and depression a person already feels. However, the outdoors encourages patients to take responsibility for themselves as well as others. Outdoors, one's behavior yields direct, immediate consequences. For example, when setting up a tent in the face of an impending storm, cooperation between partners produces results (the tent goes up faster), as does following staff instructions (the tent is set up where drainage is good).

Studies have shown that adolescents are often difficult to treat in outpatient counseling (Miller, Rathus, & Linehan, 2007). For the process of counseling to be successful, most approaches require the client to be reflective, verbal, and willing to talk and share. Many adolescents in need of counseling find this difficult and are unwilling to openly share. Some come from families where communication is problematic, making for strained dialogue in the therapist's office. Others are reluctant to see a "therapist" because of issues of trust or because they feel forced into counseling by their parents. One great way to get back at their parents for forcing the counseling issue is to refuse to talk in the session. Two other difficulties commonly encountered by adolescents in counseling involve time and treatment setting. First, most outpatient counseling occurs in 45- or 50-minute blocks of time, in an office, once a week. This type of arrangement doesn't foster the growth of an adolescent who needs time to learn to trust a therapist or who needs a more intensive therapy experience than these relatively short, infrequent sessions can provide. Second, many adolescents have grown up in a dysfunctional environment where their behavior is seen as normal. Thus, they are unable to see that they have problems, primarily because their behavior is maintained by their environment. Helping this kind of adolescent acknowledge his/her behavior and accept personal responsibility for themselves may indeed take time. Group approaches where the teenager can see the behaviors of others and receive group feedback can help him/her evaluate his/her own functioning.

Traditional outpatient approaches to therapy sometimes encourage the same kind of submissive, passive response that can develop in inpatient settings. Here, some adolescents come to view therapy as a passive process, directed and controlled by the thoughts and ideas of the therapist. This passivity is inconsistent with the need of adolescents to develop an active individual identity (Erikson, 1968). To give such power and control to a therapist has the potential to undermine the adolescent's confidence in his/her own ability to make decisions and to play a role in change. (See Figure 1.1 for questions parents and professionals can ask in deciding which treatment approach is most appropriate.)

Is the adolescent struggling with symptoms of a mental health disorder?

Has the adolescent made progress in traditional therapy?

Could the adolescent benefit from an action-oriented approach?

Would the adolescent benefit from facing some of the challenges of a wilderness environment?

Figure 1.1 **Important questions.**

The Relationship Between Therapy & Environment

The use of an outdoor setting with a group of adolescents, utilizing adventure-based activities and group therapy over a number of days, can overcome many of the limitations of traditional approaches to treatment discussed previously. This wilderness therapy experience can be simultaneously more intense than treatment in most outpatient settings and less restrictive than treatment in inpatient settings. It separates participants from environments that are likely to foster and maintain dysfunctional behavior. It is action oriented, provides immediate feedback, and emphasizes personal responsibility. At the same time, it depends on interdependence among group members and staff, promoting the development of therapeutic relationships.

What Is Wilderness?

Prior to discussing wilderness therapy itself, it is important to say a few words about the definition of wilderness itself. Do wilderness therapy programs all take place in remote, inaccessible areas? What kinds of environments can be considered wilderness? Some refer to wilderness in a very literal sense, focusing on the land and the actual characteristics of that land. Marshall (1930, p. 141) is often cited in his descriptions of wilderness as a place where "any one who lives in it has to depend exclusively on his own effort for survival; and second, that it preserves as nearly as possible the primitive environment."

The Wilderness Act of 1964 (Public Law 88-577), enacted by the United States Congress, defines wilderness as:

> An area where the earth and its community of life are untrammeled
> by man, where man himself is a visitor who does not remain....(1)
> [It] appears to have been affected primarily by the forces of nature,
> with the imprint of man's work substantially unnoticeable; (2) has
> outstanding opportunities for solitude or a primitive and uncon-
> fined type of recreation; (3) ...is of sufficient size...; (4) may also
> contain ecological, geological, or other features of scientific,
> educational, scenic, or historical value.   (U.S. Congress, 1964)

Attempts have also been made to define wilderness in terms of inner experience. Brown (1982, p. xi) talks about wilderness in this way:

> Wilderness as a modern term is relative. To the white man when he
> first came to this country, wilderness was anything that wasn't
> directly under his control. The wilderness was full of savages and
> wild beasts. When I use the term "wilderness," I use it as a conven-
> ient reference but I don't believe that land uninhabited by man is
> "wild." That kind of land is actually "natural."

Brown clearly indicates the psychological experience he looks for in this "natural" land when he says, "Seek the wilderness, for there is peace" (1982, p. xvi). Scott (1974), writing about the "psychology of wilderness experience," makes reference to altered states of consciousness and peak experiences as characteristics of wilderness. This approach suggests that, besides the untrammeled earth where people are visitors, other environments may also enhance personal growth, provide a sense of solitude, and help one find peace.

When we refer to wilderness, we do so with both literal and psychological definitions in mind. To explain this further, we accept definitions, like those of Marshall and the Wilderness Act, as defining some, but not all, of the environments that can create the positive effects of the wilderness. Other times, areas that are not so remote can provide the backdrop for the healing essence of wilderness. Any outdoor environment that fosters positive change and allows one to gain a sense of peace can be an acceptable location for wilderness therapy, but it is probably easier to find a place of this sort in unspoiled, natural environments where one can get away from the urban, crowded, mechanized world.

What Is Wilderness Therapy?

Some believe that therapy can only happen in the traditional confines of clinics, offices, and hospitals. We believe that psychotherapy involves attention to goals, in a movement toward planned change within a professional relationship (Rogers, 1957). Given this perspective on therapy, we argue that it can take place in a number of settings (Davis-Berman & Berman, 1994).

There has been a great deal of debate in the literature about definitions of wilderness therapy and therapeutic wilderness programs. These debates continue to be important for the broader field and have been discussed internationally (Bandoroff & Newes, 2003). In his writings on the topic, Williams (2004) suggests that it is important to differentiate between programs that provide therapy and those that are therapeutic for a number of reasons. First, the terms used should accurately reflect the program. Second, clients should be informed about the exact nature of a program. If it isn't therapy, they shouldn't be told it is. Third, there are ethical implications to misrepresenting the intent of a program. And fourth, by more clearly differentiating between what is therapy and what is therapeutic, we promote the professional identity of the wilderness therapy field.

Williams (2004) suggests, and we agree, that therapy programs are based in identified or diagnosed problems, and that therapeutic programs are not. Therapy programs involve specific techniques geared toward certain outcomes related to those problems. Therapeutic programs, on the other hand, are more generalized and do not need a theoretical perspective. Therapy programs are guided by theory and evaluated by research. Finally, therapy programs use trained therapists, while therapeutic programs do not. Our intent in this book is not to discuss therapeutic wilderness programs, but rather to focus on programs for which the main goal is therapy. We will use the following definition and commentary on wilderness therapy that we developed more than 10 years ago as we developed our wilderness therapy program. We believe that this conception of wilderness therapy has weathered many storms and is still relevant today. Wilderness therapy involves:

The use of traditional therapy techniques, especially those for group
therapy, in outdoor settings, utilizing outdoor adventure pursuits
and other activities to enhance growth. Wilderness therapy is a
methodical, planned approach to working with troubled youth.

(Davis-Berman & Berman, 1994, p. 13)

In this model, participants are carefully selected, based on an in-depth clinical assessment performed by a licensed mental health professional. Following this assessment, clinical treatment plans are developed for each participant, stating treatment goals and objectives. Ideally, these treatment plans are written with input from the adolescent, parent and/or guardian, and the mental health professional. Group and individual therapy is the heart of the wilderness therapy program. This therapy should be provided by qualified and fully licensed mental health professionals. Russell and Phillips-Miller (2002) add that an evaluation and aftercare component should always be part of any wilderness therapy program.

Part of our definition and conception of wilderness therapy is that in addition to the use of wilderness environments, wilderness therapy often involves outdoor, recreational and/or adventure education activities. We might use backpacking or sea kayaking, for example, as the modality with which we experience the wilderness environment. While in that setting, we might use team-building experiences or other physical challenges as adjuncts to therapy. These activities, however therapeutic and growth enhancing they may be, are not substitutes for our individual and group therapy sessions. They are activities that can facilitate communication, teamwork, and cooperation. They can also be used as a vehicle for fun, action, and interaction. However, they are not, by themselves, considered therapy. Because we will not discuss these various adventure based activities in depth, the interested reader is referred to some recent publications in the field that describe adventure activities, initiatives, and games (Rohnke, 2002; 2004a; 2004b; Snow, 2000).

Finally, in our wilderness therapy program, we try to eliminate real dangers and uncertain outcomes for two reasons: First, we believe change occurs most readily when people feel safe; also, we don't want to expose our clients to unnecessary risks. Instead, we believe that personal change can be stimulated by introducing activities in which there are some perceived risks but a very low probability of actual physical harm. Issues of safety and risk are addressed extensively in Chapter 5.

Overview of Subsequent Chapters

In Chapter 2, we look briefly at the foundation of wilderness therapy in the United States. Beginning with the tent therapy programs in the early 1900s, we discuss the development of early wilderness programs as a consequence of the love of and fascination with the wilderness.

Chapter 3 provides an overview of the current state of the field. In it, we review popular media and Internet depictions of wilderness therapy, with the goal of teaching readers to distinguish between what are accurate and truthful portrayals of the field and what are inaccurate or embellished representations.

The chapters up to this point do not address why wilderness therapy programs might be effective for certain adolescents. Chapter 4 takes a look at theoretical ideas as they relate to change in wilderness therapy programs. In easy-to-understand language, we present how and why the wilderness can be a therapeutic environment. We then mention some models of change that emphasize the perception of risk. Finally, we suggest our own ideas about change coming from safety and stability. We think that it is important to have at least some understanding of the theory behind wilderness therapy in order to be able to effectively compare it with other treatment approaches.

Chapter 5 addresses many important issues to consider about wilderness therapy. In this chapter we deal with safety, regulation, credentialing, and accreditation. We discuss these issues and, when appropriate, identify key organizations. This chapter is especially useful in learning how to evaluate and scrutinize programs.

By this point in the book, we hope that you are intrigued about the possibility of exploring a wilderness therapy program and learning more about these types of programs. In order to fully understand and appreciate these programs, it is important to address the question of treatment effectiveness. Chapter 6 talks about research and some of the unique challenges in doing research on wilderness therapy programs. Using nontechnical language, we review some recent research on the effectiveness of wilderness therapy programs.

Chapter 7 provides an overview of the variety of wilderness therapy programs, as well as general information about how programs are structured, which can be helpful in selecting a program. Because there is a great deal of overlap between different types of programs, it can be difficult to categorize them. Within this book, we talk about expedition-type wilderness therapy programs, court-related wilderness programs, and residential programs with wilderness components.

In Chapter 8 we discuss the process of choosing a wilderness therapy program. Using a question-and-answer format, we examine personal concerns of the parent, family, and adolescent. We then turn to program concerns, identifying aspects of wilderness therapy programs that are essential to understand, such as staffing, safety plans, and other crucial components.

Chapter 9 wraps up the book with a presentation and discussion of two sample cases, one in which wilderness therapy was not effective, and another where it was an effective treatment choice. We end the book with some of our own musings about the promise of wilderness therapy.

We invite you to continue reading. Not unlike a wilderness trip, we have planned our trip and know our itinerary. We sincerely hope that the chapters ahead may help you learn more about wilderness therapy as a treatment alternative for adolescents. We have been involved in this field as practitioners and researchers since the 1980s. Our commitment to wilderness therapy continues to grow and evolve. We are pleased to share some of our recent thoughts with you.

References

American Psychiatric Association. (1994). *Diagnostic and statistical manual of mental disorders* (4th ed.). Washington, D.C.: American Psychiatric Association.

Bandoroff, S., & Newes, S. (Eds.). (2003). *Coming of age: The evolving field of adventure therapy.* Boulder, CO: The Association for Experiential Education.

Berman, D., & Anton, M. (1988). A wilderness therapy program as an alternative to adolescent psychiatric hospitalization. *Residential Treatment for Children & Youth, 5,* 41–53.

Brandenburg, N., Friedman, R., & Silver, R. (1990). The epidemiology of childhood psychiatric disorders: Prevalence findings from recent studies. *Journal of the American Academy of Child & Adolescent Psychiatry, 29,* 76–83.

Breggin, P. (2000). *Reclaiming our children: The healing solution for a nation in crisis.* New York: Perseus Books.

Bridge, S., Iyengar, S., Salary, C., Barbe, R., Birmaher, B., Pincus, H., Ren, L., & Brent, D. (2007). Clinical response and risk for reported suicide attempts in pediatric antidepressant treatment: A meta-analysis of randomized controlled trials. *JAMA, 297* (15), 1683–1696.

Brown, T. (1982). *The search: The continuing story of the tracker.* New York: Berkley Books.

Brown University, (2005). Experts discuss complete review of published, unpublished data on SSRI use in children. *Child & Adolescent Psychopharmacology Update, 7* (12), 1–3.

www.Childstats.com

Davis-Berman, J., & Berman, D. (1994). *Wilderness therapy: Foundations, theory and research.* Dubuque, IA: Kendall Hunt.

Earley, P. (2006). *Crazy: A father's search through America's mental health madness.* New York: G. P. Putnam.

Erikson, E. H. (1968). *Identity: Youth & crisis.* New York: Norton.

Hampton, T. (2004). Suicide caution stamped on antidepressants. *JAMA, 291,* 2060–2061.

www.hhs.gov

Johnson, L., O'Malley, P., & Bachman, J. (2003). *Monitoring the future: National results on adolescent drug use: Overview of key findings.* (NIH Publication No. 03-5374). Bethesda, MD. National Institute on Drug Abuse.

Johnson, L., O'Malley, P., Bachman, J., & Schulenberg, J. (2005). *Monitoring the future: National results on alcohol drug abuse, overview of findings, 2004.* Bethesda, MD: National Institute on Drug Abuse.

Juszczak, L., Melinkovich, P., & Kaplan, D. (2003). Use of health and mental health services by adolescents across multiple delivery sites. *Journal of Adolescent Health*, 32, 108–118.

Kazdin, A. (1989). Developmental psychopathology: Current research, issues, and directions. *American Psychologist*, 44, 180–187.

Kozol, J. (1991). *Savage inequalities*. New York: Harper Perennial.

Kozol, J. (1995). *Amazing grace*. New York: Harper Collins.

Kozol, J. (2000). *Ordinary resurrections*. New York: Harper Collins.

Kozol, J. (2005). *The shame of the nation: The restoration of Apartheid schooling in America*. New York: Crown Publishing.

Marshall, R. (1930). The problem of the wilderness. *Scientific Monthly*, 30, 141–147.

Miller, L. (2000, March 9). Kids on drugs: A behavioral pediatrician questions the wisdom of medicating our children. Retrieved October 25, 2005 from http://www.salon.com/health.

Miller, A., Rathus, J., & Linehan, M. (2007). *Dialectical behavior therapy with suicidal adolescents*. New York: Guilford Press.

Murray, M., deVries, C., & Wong, I. (2004). A drug utilization study of anti-depressants in children and adolescents using the General Practice Research Database. *Archives of Disease in Childhood*, 89, 1098–1102.

Ponton, L. (1997). *The romance of risk: Why teenagers do the things they do*. New York: BasicBooks.

Raeburn, P. (2004). *Acquainted with the night: A parent's quest to understand depression and bipolar disorder in his children*. New York: Broadway Books.

Rogers, C. (1957). The necessary and sufficient conditions of therapeutic personality change. *Journal of Consulting and Clinical Psychology*, 21, 95–103.

Rohnke, K. (2002). *A small book about large group games*. Dubuque, IA: Kendall Hunt.

Rohnke, K. (2004a). *The bottomless bag revival*. Dubuque, IA: Kendall Hunt.

Rohnke, K. (2004b). *Funn 'n games*. Dubuque, IA: Kendall Hunt.

Russell, K., & Phillips-Miller, D. (2002). Perspectives on the wilderness therapy process and its relation to outcome. *Child & Youth Care Forum*, 31, 415–437.

SAMHSA, (2006). OAS Reports: A day in the life of american adolescents: Substance use facts. Retrieved on November 5, 2007 from www.oas.samhsa.gov.

Scott, N. R. (1974). Wilderness experience. *Natural Resources Journal*, 14, 231–237.

Seligman, M. E. (1975). *Helplessness: On depression, development and death*. San Francisco: W. H. Freeman.

Snow, H. (2000). *Indoor/outdoor team building games for trainers: Powerful activities from the world of adventure based team building and ropes courses*. New York: McGraw-Hill.

Tuma, J. (1989). Mental health services for children: The state of the art. *American Psychologist*, 44, 188–199.

UNICEF. (2005). *The state of the world's children 2005: Childhood under threat*. New York.

U.S. Congress. (1964). *Wilderness act*. Public Law 88–577.

U.S. Department of Health and Human Services (1999). *Surgeon general's report on mental health*. Rockville, MD.

U.S. Department of Health and Human Services (2001). *Youth violence: A report of the surgeon general*. Rockville, MD.

Varley, C. (2006). Treating depression in children and adolescents: What options now?. *CNS Drugs*, 20 (1), 1–13.

Vasa, R., Carlino, A., & Pine, D. (2006). Pharmacotherapy of depressed children and adolescents: Current issues and potential directions, *Biological Psychiatry*, 59(11), 1021–1028.

Williams, I. (2004). Adventure therapy or therapeutic adventure? In S. Bandoroff & S. Newes (Eds.), *Coming of age: The evolving field of adventure therapy* (pp. 195–208). Boulder, CO: Association for Experiential Education.

CHAPTER 2

A Brief History

In the summer of 1901, the *American Journal of Insanity* reported that psychiatric patients with tuberculosis were placed in tents on the grounds of the Manhattan State Hospital East in New York (Wright & Haviland, 1903). This wasn't done with any therapeutic intentions in mind; rather, it was done to prevent them from infecting the other patients in the hospital. While some of those in the advanced stages of tuberculosis died, dramatic improvements were seen in the remaining patients. Not only did their physical health improve, their mental attitudes and outlooks also improved significantly. After the summer season, some of the patients returned to the wards and their old routines. This was necessary due to the lack of equipment with which to heat the outdoor areas. As a result, many patients regressed in their behaviors, and once again became incontinent and withdrawn. The majority of those who stayed in tents throughout the winter, however, continued to improve (Caplan, 1974).

Critical space problems at the hospital and the improvement in the tubercular patients led to the suggestion that other patients be included during the second year of the tenting program (Wright & Haviland, 1903). Thus, nontubercular psychiatric patients were put into tents. Once again, fairly dramatic physical and psychiatric improvements were seen. Most patients gained weight, began to control destructive behaviors, and even gained control over their bladder problems. Some even improved to the point of being discharged from the hospital. Commenting on the effectiveness of this program, Wright & Haviland (1903, p. 59) said, "We consider the results obtained with camp treatment to be of such character as to warrant us in employing it as a practical therapeutic measure in the modern treatment of the insane."

The early use of tents in psychiatric hospitals was not limited to Manhattan State Hospital East. In fact, shortly after the San Francisco earthquake of 1906, psychiatric patients from the Agnew Asylum were housed in tents (Caplan, 1974). In a letter Dr. Andrew Hoisholt wrote to the editors of the *American Journal of Insanity* he said: "Patients [of Agnew Asylum] who had been more or less constantly violent and untidy when confined in the building were now getting along peacefully. They all seemed more comfortable and contented in the tents and on the open grounds" (Hoisholt, 1906, p. 131).

Another issue of the journal describes a camp on the Susquehanna River for patients from Binghamton State Hospital. It was thought by the staff that this summer camping program was a "valuable part of the treatment of the recoverable patients" (*American Journal of Insanity*, 1910, p. 445). A summer camp program, although in cottages instead of tents, was offered in New York at the Bloomingdale Hospital in White Plains. The benefits of this program are described most effectively by the words of a patient who said: "The beach cottage part of the summer of 1915 was the beginning of my improvement, and we all felt that it was the lift we otherwise would not have had" (*American Journal of Insanity*, 1916, p. 334).

This tent therapy movement came to life within a larger context of philosophical and cultural change in the United States. In the mid-1800s, the mental hygiene movement was born, largely in response to what was seen as the inhumane treatment of patients in mental hospitals. Reformers revolted against the conditions, even suggesting that hospitalizing patients with mental illnesses might not be the best treatment. In 1880, the National Association for the Protection of the Insane was formed as part of the movement (Moniz & Gorin, 2007). Later, in 1908, Clifford Beers wrote *A Mind that Found Itself*, his expose of his own experience as a patient in a hospital (Beers, 1908), establishing him as a leader in the mental hygiene movement.

In the mid-19th century, reformers also began to advocate for treatment of patients outside of hospital settings. In 1841, Dorthea Dix, a school teacher, began to work for the improvement of conditions in institutions for the mentally ill. She wrote a document that was presented to the Massachusetts legislature, resulting in increased funding for state hospitals in that state. In addition to being a key player in the revolt against conditions in hospitals, she was also convinced that community-based treatment was more effective than hospitalization. Her ideas about the impact of social factors in causing mental illnesses and her public advocacy efforts reached the national level and were pivotal in the eventual formation of the American Psychological Association.

Finally, in the 1880s, reformers like Jane Adams fought to open the community to those in need of treatment. Her approach, which is still used today, was to place centers for treatment in neighborhoods, where people in need could obtain service and community support (Tausig & Subedi, 2004). This mental hygiene movement was defined by a less harsh, more compassionate view of mental illness and treatment.

At the same time, a more positive view of the wilderness was evolving. Ideas about the wilderness as a harsh and unforgiving place that needed to be conquered were replaced with romantic sentiments. The wilderness was beginning to be seen as an environment to retreat to, to engage with, and to draw healing from (Nash, 1967). These sentiments were expressed aptly in travelogues, monthly magazines, and novels and poems. Some of the greatest writers of the time, including Henry Wadsworth Longfellow, Walt Whitman, and Henry David Thoreau also extolled the virtues of the wilderness.

For example, in the "Song of Myself " Whitman wrote about the peace he found by leaving civilization behind as he hunted, then fell peacefully asleep on the leaves. He also presented idyllic images of the wilderness areas in the West, as he wrote about happiness in the open air in "Song of the Open Road" (Whitman, 1940). Probably most recognized are the writings of Henry David Thoreau, in which he wrote about his retreats to Walden Pond: "I went to the woods because I wished to live deliberately, to front only the essential facts of life, and see if I could not learn what it had to teach, and not, when I came to die, discover that I had not lived" (Thoreau, 1960, p. 66).

The art of the time also reflected this positive conception of wilderness. Paintings by artists like Frederic Church and Albert Bierstadt portrayed the natural environment in all its beauty and majesty (Nash, 1967; Rosenblum, 1975). With literature and art presenting images of sunlight, warmth and allure, it is not surprising that the wilderness began to be seen not as a place to be conquered, but as a place of rest and rejuvenation. These literary and artistic portrayals of a benevolent wilderness boosted popular affinity for the wilderness, which in turn increased government interest in the preservation of wilderness lands. As a result, starting in the late 1800s and through the first part of the next century, wilderness areas were protected, and preservationist organizations like the Sierra Club were formed (Nash, 1967).

With the approach of World War I, attention to the healing elements of the wilderness was relegated to the back burner. During the war, the *American Journal of Insanity* shifted its focus from articles about treatments for the mentally ill to discussions about combat and troops. When the *American Journal of Insanity* became the *American Journal of Psychiatry* in 1920, newsy articles, like the tent therapy articles, totally disappeared (Caplan, 1974). The use of the outdoors as a treatment setting did not reemerge until almost a decade later, with the development of the therapeutic camping movement.

The Origins of Therapeutic Camps

The first recorded use of a camp as a venue with the capacity for effecting social change in youth was at Camp Ahmek in Canada's Algonquin Park. Established in 1929, Ahmek was the first recreational camp for boys to identify socialization of a camper's behavior as a goal (Dimock & Hendry, 1939). The program used the power of the group and the role modeling of the staff to encourage cooperation and positive behavior. Leaders were especially tuned into the natural environment and how cooperation in this environment was essential to success in the program. Although therapeutic in its focus, Camp Ahmek did not cater to young people with mental health problems.

Then, around the mid-1900s, camping therapy programs developed. The Fresh Air Camp, developed by the University of Michigan, only served campers suffering from mental health problems. Its programming relied heavily on psychiatric diagnosis, observation, and psychotherapy and, in addition to trained counselors, staff psychologists were used on a regular basis (Morse, 1957).

The Salesmanship Club of Dallas is another example of an early program designed to be therapeutic. The camp was first developed in 1946 as a summer camp, originally called Camp Woodland Springs. Two years later, the camp became a year-round program, focused on meeting the needs of boys with emotional problems (Smith, 1958). Led for two decades by Campbell Loughmiller, The Salesmanship Club relied heavily on the power of the wilderness environment and the natural consequences inherent in this environment (Loughmiller, 1965). These ideas form the foundation of many wilderness therapy programs today. In fact, the Salesmanship Club of Dallas still exists as a rather large social service organization. Instead of a residential camp program, it now offers some expedition camping programs for youth.

Outward Bound

One cannot discuss relatively modern wilderness programs without spending some time on the development and implementation of Outward Bound, as this program, from its outset, has stressed personal growth and development. The birth of Outward Bound occurred in 1941 in Aberdovey, Wales. It was the brainchild of Kurt Hahn (the headmaster of a Scottish school) and Lawrence Holt (who actually named the school Outward Bound) (Miner & Boldt, 1981).

As an educator, Hahn had been working on a plan to help improve the physical fitness of British youth. At the same time, Holt, who was involved in a merchant shipping company, noticed that many of the young, physically fit British seamen were not surviving conditions at sea as well as some of the older, less fit men. This observation led the two men to collaborate, and they started a new school where the focus on fitness and mental attitude would carry on to all parts of life. The belief behind the school's focus was that bolstering both the physical and psychological components of the individual would facilitate his/her ability to cope with difficult and demanding situations and conditions (Katz & Kolb, 1967; Stich & Gaylor, 1983).

Two early Outward Bound studies that involved adolescents led the way for later therapeutic research and program development. One study suggested that delinquents who participated in an Outward Bound program experienced lower recidivism (reoffense) rates after treatment than did participants in traditional treatment programs (Kelly & Baer, 1968). Sixty delinquents enrolled at Outward Bound were compared with a control group of 60 boys. Nine months after treatment ended, the recidivism rate for the Outward Bound group was 20%, as compared to 34% for the control group. Also, the Outward Bound group showed positive change in alienation, asocial behavior, and aggression (Kelly & Baer, 1968).

The second study evaluated the effectiveness of the Colorado Outward Bound School's programs. Fifty adolescent participants completed a self-rating scale, a self-description, an ideal description, and a word-meaning test. These measures were given at arrival, before the program and after the program ended. The results suggested that the participants improved in their self-images, especially those who had low self-esteem to begin with (Clifford & Clifford, 1967).

These two studies are very important because they used accepted research principles. They also suggested that Outward Bound programming could be successfully applied to at-risk populations. The idea that at-risk or somehow troubled adolescents could be helped by Outward Bound no doubt encouraged the development of programs more directly geared toward participants with psychiatric problems. For example, the Hurricane Island Outward Bound School sponsored a mental health project that was affiliated with Dartmouth Medical School. Psychiatric patients were taken on a short wilderness expedition led by Outward Bound staff (Stich & Senior, 1984). Presently, Outward Bound has programs for adjudicated youth in Florida and South Carolina, as well as programs for other at-risk youth. Although Outward Bound is not known as a wilderness therapy program, it currently offers its Intercept program. Not advertised as a therapeutic program, this offering is geared toward troubled teens exhibiting "challenging behaviors" (www.outwardbound.org).

Although a pivotal and well-known force behind the use of wilderness as a therapeutic setting, Outward Bound is not the only modern program to do so. Some psychiatric day treatment programs used the outdoors to therapeutic ends (Reitman & Pokorney, 1974), as did other more traditional psychiatric hospital programs (Ackerman, Mitsos, Seymour, & Smith, 1974; Remar & Lowry, 1974; McDonald, 1974). An interesting example occurred at Boston State Hospital, where a camping program for patients operated from 1966 to 1972. The camping component involved chronic psychiatric patients and usually involved an eight-night camping experience. Although no formal evaluation data was collected, patient reactions to the experience tended to be quite positive. Staff also reported that the program was good for not only the patients, but for them as well (Remar & Lowry, 1974). At the Oregon State Hospital, an equal number of patients and staff went on a two-week camping trip. This experience, which occurred about six months into the traditional hospital stay, consisted of rafting, hiking, and climbing experiences. In the words of one of the patients after completing a difficult rock climbing experience, "If I can do this, I can solve my own problems, can't I?" (McDonald, 1974, p. 30). These programs for psychiatric patients paved the way for other expedition programs, setting the stage for more refined offerings for psychiatric inpatients and outpatients (e.g., Berman & Anton, 1988; Davis-Berman & Berman, 1991, 1994b).

Until 1970, the number of programs that used the wilderness in a therapeutic manner was small. The decades of the 1970s and 1980s saw a significant growth of programs based in outdoor settings geared toward working with youth. While many of those programs are still around, others were only viable for a short time. In Chapter 7 we present a current description of numerous modern wilderness therapy programs. We also provide information about court-related and residential programs with strong wilderness components.

The Professionalization of the Field

As new programs developed, professionals began to gather to provide support and direction to each other. Eventually, informal networking led to the development of important professional associations that are still in operation today. Some of these associations offer accreditation services, while others suggest standards and ethical codes of conduct.

In the early 1970s, a group of outdoor professionals formed the first association specifically for professionals who used the outdoors in their work with clients. Named the Association for Experiential Education (AEE, the publisher of this book), it started out as a membership organization whose primary function was networking, professional development (through conferences), and the sharing of research and ideas (through a journal). Through the years, it has evolved and is now a major accrediting organization of outdoor programs.

Issues surrounding the regulation and evaluation of programs began to arise in the 1970s. The establishment of the VisionQuest program for adjudicated youth in the early 1970s, for example, prompted the state of Arizona to begin to examine and draft standards for residential programs. At the same time other programs, like Anasazi, began to work on strategizing about ways to obtain insurance reimbursement (Russell, 2001). These programs are discussed in Chapter 7.

It was in the 1990s, however, that the professionalization of wilderness therapy programs really came into its own. The National Association of Therapeutic Wilderness Camps (NATWC) was formed in 1994, with the intention of representing the therapeutic camping field and enhancing practice through education and networking (www.natwc.org). In addition, NATWC now offers a counselor recognition program for qualified counselors in wilderness programs. Then, in 1996, The Outdoor Behavioral Healthcare Industry Council (OBHIC) was formed to set standards in the field of wilderness therapy, promoting unity and support among programs that share similar philosophies and operating standards. OBHIC has also played a role helping wilderness therapy programs gain acceptance as legitimate, reimbursable health care programs (www.obhic.com). In 1999, out of OBHIC's commitment to research on the process and effectiveness of wilderness therapy programs, grew the Outdoor Behavioral Healthcare Research Cooperative (OBHRC). (See Chapter 6 for information about some of the research conducted by OBHRC.) Also in 1999, the National Association of Therapeutic Schools and Programs (NATSAP) was founded with the intent of serving as a resource for outdoor programs and professionals (www.natsap.org). These organizations have been critical to the development of wilderness therapy programs and are discussed in more detail in Chapter 5.

Chapter 3 discusses public perspectives of wilderness therapy as seen through the Internet and in other media outlets. We also present material on boot camps, as these programs are often portrayed in the popular media. This is important information in that parents and clinicians should be aware of the veracity of the various images and messages to which they are exposed. The chapter ends with some guidance on how to decide if a wilderness therapy program is the right choice for your child or client.

References

Ackerman, O., Mitsos, S., Seymour, M., & Smith, B. (1974). Some camping therapy programs in Indiana and Texas. In T.P. Lowry (Ed.). *Camping therapy: Its uses in psychiatry and rehabilitation*, pp. 39–45. Springfield, IL: Charles C. Thomas.

American Journal of Insanity. (1910).

American Journal of Insanity. (1916).

Beers, C. (1908). *A mind that found itself*. New York: American Foundation for Mental Hygiene.

Berman D., & Anton, M. (1988). Wilderness therapy as an alternative to adolescent psychiatric hospitalization. *Residential Treatment for Children and Youth, 5*, 39–52.

Caplan, R. (1974). Early forms of camping in American mental hospitals. In T.P. Lowry (Ed.), *Camping therapy: Its uses in psychiatry and rehabilitation*, pp. 8–12. Springfield, IL: Charles C. Thomas.

Clifford, E., & Clifford, M. (1967). Self-concept before and after survival training. *British Journal of Social and Clinical Psychology, 6*, 241–248.

Davis-Berman, J., & Berman, D. (1991). The Wilderness Therapy Program: An empirical study of its effects with adolescents in an outpatient setting. *Journal of Contemporary Psychotherapy, 19*, 271–281.

Davis-Berman, J., & Berman, D. (1994a). *Wilderness therapy: Foundations, theory and research*. Dubuque, IA: Kendall Hunt.

Davis-Berman, J., & Berman, D. (1994b). Research update: Two-year follow-up report for the Wilderness Therapy Program. *Journal of Experiential Education, 17*(1), 48–50.

Dimock, H., & Hendry, C. (1939). *Camping and character: A camp experiment in character education*. New York: Association Press.

Hoisholt, A. (1906). Letter to the editors. *American Journal of Insanity, 63*, 131–132.

Kelly, F., & Baer, D. (1968). *Outward Bound schools as an alternative to institutionalization for adolescent delinquent boys*. Boston: Fandel Press.

Katz, R., & Kolb, D. (1967). *Outward Bound and education for personal growth*. Reston, VA: Outward Bound.

Loughmiller, C. (1965). *Wilderness road*. Austin, TX: Hogg Foundation for Mental Health.

McDonald, M. (1974). Adventure camping at Oregon State Hospital. In T.P. Lowry (Ed.). *Camping therapy: Its uses in psychiatry and rehabilitation*, pp. 16–31. Springfield, IL: Charles C. Thomas.

Miner, J., & Boldt, J. (1981). *Outward Bound USA: Learning through experience in adventure based education*. New York: William Morrow & Co.

Moniz, C., & Gorin, S. (2007). *Health and mental health care policy: A biopsychosocial perspective.* Boston: Pearson Education.

Morse, W. (1957). An interdisciplinary therapeutic camp. *Journal of Social Issues, 13*(1), 15–22.

Nash, R. (1967). *Wilderness and the American mind.* New Haven, CT: Yale University Press.

www.natsap.org

www.natwc.org

www.obhic.org

www.outwardbound.org

Reitman, E., & Pokorney, A. (1974). Camping at a psychiatric day center. In T.P. Lowry (Ed.). *Camping therapy: Its uses in psychiatry and rehabilitation,* pp. 63–67. Springfield, IL: Charles C. Thomas.

Remar, E., & Lowry, T. (1974). Camping therapy in the commonwealth of Massachusetts. In T. P. Lowry (Ed.). *Camping therapy: Its uses in psychiatry and rehabilitation,* pp. 13–15. Springfield, IL: Charles C. Thomas.

Rosenblum, R. (1975). *Modern painting and the northern romantic tradition: Friedrich to Rothko.* New York: Harper & Row.

Russell, K. (2001). What is wilderness therapy? *Journal of Experiential Education, 24*(2), 70–79.

Smith, B. (1958). *The worth of a boy.* Austin, TX: The Hogg Foundation for Mental Health.

Stich, T., & Gaylor, M. (1983). Outward Bound: An innovative patient education program. Eric Document Reproduction Service No. ED247047, 1–18.

Stich, T., & Senior, N. (1984). Adventure therapy: An innovative treatment for psychiatric patients. In B. Pepper & H. Ryglewicz (Eds.). *Advances in training the young adult chronic patient: New directions in mental health services,* No.21. San Francisco: Jossey-Bass.

Tausig, M., & Subedi, S. (2004). *A sociology of mental illness.* 2nd Ed. New Jersey: Prentice Hall.

Thoreau, H. (1960). *Walden and "civil disobedience."* New York: New American Library.

Whitman, W. (1940). *Leaves of Grass.* Garden City, NY: Doubleday, Doran (Originally published 1855).

Wright, A., & Haviland, C. (1903). Additional notes upon tent treatment for the insane at the Manhattan State Hospital East, *American Journal of Insanity, 60,* 53–59.

CHAPTER 3

The Current State of the Field: Perception Versus Reality

So much of what we see and hear these days comes through sensationalized sources, such as television and the Internet. Unfortunately, a lot of the information that we accept as fact is often actually some blend of truth and fiction. In this chapter, we discuss portrayals of wilderness programs that you might have seen on television or read about in magazines and might have been confused about or wanted to know more about.

We also provide an overview of a few Internet sites that may be of interest to those exploring this field. While the Internet is loaded with great information, it has an equal if not greater amount of misinformation. Finally, we also discuss boot camps, because they are the types of programs most frequently portrayed and discussed in the media, especially on daytime television.

Using the Internet to Your Advantage

The Internet is a logical place to begin when researching wilderness therapy programs, but we must issue a warning: A vast amount of information on wilderness therapy has been posted on the Internet, and although some of it is helpful and valid, much of it is unsupported. A recent inquiry about wilderness therapy on a popular search engine yielded 1,360,000 responses. (Talk about information overload!) Many of the results were direct links to wilderness therapy program websites. Almost always, such websites only provide general information and not many details about the actual structure of the program. Sometimes, programs present themselves in ways that are not completely true (i.e., they may imply that their therapists are with the participants at all times when, in fact, therapists only see participants once a week). In the interest of getting the whole truth, we strongly recommend you use the Internet as a starting point, and then, once you've identified a program of interest, follow up by phone or, ideally, in person.

One last word of warning about the Internet: You're bound to encounter something called "sponsored links." You may also find entries like "The Best Four Sites in Wilderness Therapy." When interpreting such claims, it is important to bear in mind that sponsored links are paid advertisements and should be understood as such.

Unfortunately, there is no single website that serves as a clearing-house for all things related to wilderness therapy, so we've compiled a list of websites that—when taken as a whole—provide general information and access to a network of professionals who either practice and/or do research on the field, and forward and promote best practices for the field. The websites we recommend fall into two categories: The first category includes the websites of professional organizations (see Figure 3.1). Individually, these sites tell only part of the wilderness therapy story, but in combination they provide a broad perspective of how best practices, standards, and regulation influence wilderness therapy programming. Each of these organizations is discussed in some detail in Chapter 5, so we refer you to that chapter for more information about them.

- Association for Experiential Education: www.aee.org

- Council on Accreditation: www.coa.org

- The Joint Commission: www.jointcommission.org

- National Association of Therapeutic Schools and Programs: www.natsap.org

- National Association of Therapeutic Wilderness Camps: www.natwc.org

- Outdoor Behavioral Healthcare Industry Council: www.obhic.com

Figure 3.1 **Professional organization website URLs.**

The second category includes three sites that will feel more accessible to those new to the field. Please note that these sites are hosted by individuals and, as such, the information and links they list are not without some bias. (See Figure 3.2.)

The most comprehensive and least biased of these sites is called the Adventure Therapy and Wilderness/Nature Therapy website (www.wilderdom.com/adventuretherapy.html). Commonly referred to as wilderdom.com, this site provides both basic and advanced information regarding the fields of adventure and wilderness therapy, including definitions, discussions, and articles about history and research on wilderness therapy programs written by prominent scholars in the field, as well as links to other sites that may be helpful and are not listed here. It is hosted by James Neill, a psychologist and researcher who hails from and lives in Australia and has taught at the University of New Hampshire in the United States. His passion for disseminating information is a huge service to various fields, including wilderness therapy.

Another helpful site, called Struggling Teens (www.strugglingteens.org), is hosted by Lon Woodbury, an educational consultant. We mention this up front because as an educational consultant, Woodbury is in the business of referring clients to specific programs. As such, he has a personal agenda. That said, Woodbury is very straightforward about his profession and the website's main purpose (to match potential clients with programs).

In his capacity as an educational consultant, Woodbury stays on top of issues affecting the field, and his online newsletter includes a section on breaking news in the wilderness therapy field that can be quite insightful. He also includes an online discussion forum (moderated by another educational consultant) that can generate helpful dialogue. Forum participants can ask questions about specific programs and get answers and support from consultants and other participants. It is important to note that the programs and schools listed on strugglingteens.org are paid advertisers. However, this website also sells *The Parent Empowerment Handbook* ($50), which lists residential schools and programs in the United States. Programs included in this book are not paid advertisers, and so it is considered a more objective source of information than the list of programs who have paid for inclusion on the website.

A final note on educational consultants: The use of educational consultants as an effective tool for parents is controversial and has been questioned by some due to a lack of regulation (Pinto, Friedman, & Epstein, 2005).

Finally, there is also a site called Wilderness Therapy and Treatment (www.wilderness-therapy.org), which is hosted by Dr. Michael Conner, a licensed psychologist who practices in clinical, family, and medical psychology. Information posted on his site includes basic information about wilderness therapy, all of which is written by Dr. Conner, as well as links to other organizations that promote adventure, wilderness, and outdoor behavioral therapy (which may be the site's greatest asset). Although Dr. Conner is quick to point out that he is not affiliated with any specific wilderness therapy programs and does not accept advertising on his site, it is important to note that in his professional capacity, Dr. Conner refers clients to wilderness therapy programs. As such, some professionals in the field question whether the website is in some ways a promotional tool for the programs Dr. Conner recommends on the site. We trust that you will be able to glean from this site what is valuable to you and discern what may be Dr. Conner's biases.

- www.wilderdom.com/adventure therapy.html
  Professionally oriented site that includes access to relevant research in the field.

- www.strugglingteens.org
  Publishes an online newsletter, hosts a discussion forum, and provides links to popular media sources.

- www.wilderness-therapy.org
  Provides some background information on wilderness therapy.

Figure 3.2 **Internet sites hosted by individuals that are discussed in this chapter.**

Other Topics You May Encounter

When doing Internet research about wilderness therapy programs, reference to deaths of participants invariably arises. Although an uncomfortable reality, individuals interested in wilderness therapy programs should investigate this potential danger. An article Jon Krakauer wrote for *Outside Magazine* in 1995 makes a good starting point. "Loving Them to Death" detailed the deaths of adolescents in wilderness therapy programs in the early 1990s. It is important to note, however, that as a result of increased regulation the field has changed significantly since this article was written. Krakauer's article can be read either in the magazine (Krakauer, 1995a) or online (Krakauer, 1995b).

Other more recent articles posted on the Internet also address the risks and benefits of participating in wilderness therapy programs. Arline Kaplan, an independent writer for psychiatric publications, provides a good overview of the subject in an article she originally wrote for *Psychiatric Times*. She also specifically discusses some of the deaths that have occurred in wilderness therapy programs and provides a list of questions that could be asked of program representatives about deaths and injuries in their programs. These are important questions to consider before enrolling in a wilderness therapy program and include:

1. Is the program licensed by a state agency in an appropriate way (e.g., alcohol/drug treatment facility) and/or accredited by JCAHO [The Joint Commission], the COA [Council on Accreditation], or other accreditation organizations?

2. Are licensed clinical professionals on staff?

3. Has the staff been screened for drugs, and what types of training do they have?

4. Have there been any deaths in the program or in any program established by the organizers?

5. What happens to the kids after they leave the program?

6. Have any follow-up studies been conducted?

7. How involved are the parents in treatment process, and does the program permit child-parent contact?

8. Does the program operate out of the country?

9. Is the program a member of an industry association, such as NATSAP [National Association of Therapeutic Schools and Programs] or OBHIC [Outdoor Behavioral Healthcare Council]?

10. Will the program freely disclose the nature of its services as well as benefits, risks, and costs?

(Kaplan, 2002)

Readers interested in Kaplan's entire article can go to her website (www.healthrising.com), where she has posted not only this article but numerous others that you may find informative. While only the article referenced here focuses specifically on youth and wilderness therapy, other articles she has written about children's mental health can be accessed through the "Stories" link at her site.

If you do make it to the point of interviewing programs, we encourage you to reference the previous list of questions and to be frank when asking program representatives about injury and death rates in their programs. Don't be intimidated by a representative who tells you not to worry because wilderness therapy programs are safe. It is true that, in general, these programs are quite safe, but it is wise to investigate, ask questions, and be informed. (See Chapter 5 for a detailed discussion of the issues of risk management and its relationship to program safety.)

TV: Truth or Fiction?

The reality television phenomenon that has taken off so wildly in the United States has capitalized on the desire of many people to vicariously experience the pain and suffering of others. One such show debuted during the summer of 2005: Named "Brat Camp," it had American viewers glued to their sets. (Ironically, *Brat Camp* wasn't a new series, but most Americans had missed it the first time around, and when the media played it up during its second run, the masses tuned in).

The first season of *Brat Camp* was developed and filmed at a well-respected program (RedCliff Ascent) in the state of Utah. The original adolescent participants were selected in London, screened for appropriateness by a psychologist, and then approved for inclusion by the project executives. The major stated goal of this project was to expose parents in the United Kingdom to wilderness therapy as an alternative to traditional approaches to working with troubled teenagers. It was thought that by filming the actual program, parents would be exposed to a positive perspective on this approach and would begin to consider it as a viable treatment option.

Many meetings took place to strategize about how to create an interesting television series without compromising the integrity and effectiveness of the treatment program. Although intentions were good, some of the participants and therapists have since said that they felt that the presence of the cameras compromised the program's effectiveness. For example, participants and therapists said that they avoided some volatile issues and certain conflicts because they didn't want to be on camera dealing with certain topics. Some of the participants also admitted to "playing for the cameras," creating a soap opera–type of atmosphere that was not very therapeutic for the adolescents. Even so, *Brat Camp* was largely viewed as a success: It was entertaining and exposed the public to a new method of treatment. As for ratings, the show did well in the United Kingdom, Australia, and New Zealand, but in the U.S., the first round of *Brat Camp* aired on ABC's Family Channel and didn't get much attention.

Based on the program's success, ABC approached RedCliff Ascent about filming a second *Brat Camp*. RedCliff denied that request, due to their concerns about the impact on the integrity of their program, and the production company turned to another program in the western United States called SageWalk. In July of 2005, ABC broadcast in prime time a "new" reality series also called *Brat Camp*. This time around, U.S. viewers were riveted to the screen every week to see Lauren, Jada, Nick, Shawn, Heather, Lexie, Frank, Derek, and Isaiah struggle with issues like drug abuse, anger management, grief, depression, anxiety, and abandonment. You name it, the show featured it. Participation on the show was voluntary, all participants were aware that their wilderness therapy program would be filmed, and they agreed to be part of this process. But one key factor undermined the validity of the show: ABC paid the cost of the program for all of the participants.

Given the fact that programs often cost as much as $14,000 a month, this was a significant motivator for adolescents and their parents to agree to participate. Last but not least, the production staff at ABC had the final decision in selecting participants from a group of adolescents who had been admitted to the program (Malholland, 2005). One can assume that ABC chose participants who would be interesting and lively on camera.

Whether the *Brat Camp* series was a boon or bane to the wilderness therapy field depends on whom you ask. While it exposed the public to the process and possibilities of wilderness therapy (RedCliff Ascent's website receives more than double the hits it did pre-*Brat Camp* [Jones, 2005]), many issues and concerns about the series have been raised by wilderness therapy professionals. For example, some questioned the ethics of even airing such a program, given the confidential nature of the process of therapy. Is it exploiting the young participants to make their problems public? Although some may argue that the parents consented to their adolescents' participation, it's important to note that by footing the bill, ABC offered the parents some hope of treatment for their children that might otherwise have been financially out of their reach. Also, certain outdoor activities (such as rappelling) that were not standard elements of the program were added prior to filming to increase drama and action. Finally, many concerns were raised about the sensational way in which ABC identified the participants in the program with labels like "angry punk," "drug addict," and "compulsive liar." In the wilderness therapy field, labeling and exploiting participants for the cameras is unethical and does not provide an accurate or realistic perspective on wilderness therapy as a treatment approach. Despite these concerns, it seems that *Brat Camp* is here to stay. *Brat Camp* programs have continued to be filmed in the U.S. and aired in the United Kingdom. Programs have included a girls-only trip and a family brat camp experience. Information on the airing of these programs can be found at www.twentytwenty.tv/

Brat Camp is not the only popularized view of wilderness therapy programs depicted in the United States. Although boot camp programs are not consistent with the definition of wilderness therapy that we support, we discuss them here because many boot camps identify themselves as wilderness therapy programs. The standard in boot camps is to treat the adolescents in a punitive fashion, attempting to break participants down in order to build them back up again.

Beware Boot Camps

Boot camp programs grew out of a movement in the late 1950s in the United States to treat youth with structure, discipline, and limits. Gone were the days of spoiling and coddling young people who misbehaved. In fact, these practices were seen as contributing to adolescent misbehavior, especially drug and alcohol abuse. Early programs were geared toward adolescents in the criminal justice system, offering an alternative to incarceration. Later, programs were expanded to include adolescents with various drug addictions (Szalavitz, 2006). The approaches aimed to be scary and confrontational, as it was thought that treatment and rehabilitation required the adolescent be completely broken down before s/he could be rebuilt. With the continued popularity of these methods and with the publication of the book *Tough Love* (York, York, & Wachtel, 1982), this "tough" approach began to be used more widely and was applied to youth with a variety of behavioral issues. The failure of some of the prominent programs at this time led, in the early 1990s, to the development of boot camp wilderness programs. (A discussion of the history of these programs is beyond the scope of this book. The reader is referred to Szalavitz's [2006] book, *Help at Any Cost: How the Troubled-Teen Industry Cons Parents and Hurts Kids*, for this background, and for a thorough presentation of the development of the boot camp movement in the United States.)

Boot camp programs are known for their tough approach to working with delinquent youth. The emphasis of these types of programs is rigorous (some would say punishing) physical conditioning. They have been most popular in the juvenile justice system with their attempts to break the will of difficult youth through intimidation and humiliation. Some programs designed for at-risk youth in general, not only those in the criminal justice system, have adopted this approach. Many of these programs make use of the wilderness environment and are sometimes referred to as wilderness therapy programs. Beware of any program that uses intimidation or humiliation, even if it calls itself a wilderness therapy program. For clarification of what distinguishes wilderness therapy programs from boot camp wilderness programs, let's reiterate our definition of wilderness therapy. We have suggested that wilderness therapy involves:

> … the use of traditional therapy techniques, especially those for group therapy in outdoor settings, utilizing outdoor adventure pursuits and other activities to enhance growth. Wilderness therapy is a methodical, planned approach to working with troubled youth.

> Wilderness therapy programs strive to minimize potential physical and emotional risk to participants. In fact, we believe that personal change can be stimulated by introducing activities where

> there are some perceived risks but a very low probability of actual
> physical harm.   (Davis-Berman & Berman, 1994)

The concept of change occurring within an atmosphere of safety is a basic tenet of the psychotherapy literature tracing back as far as the work of Carl Rogers in the 1950s (Rogers, 1957). The emphasis on avoiding excessive risk is consistent with the ideas of some important thinkers in the adventure therapy field as well. For example, Denise Mitten (1999) has been quite influential in discussing the importance of being open to models of change that don't focus on risk and pushing participants outside of their zones of comfort. Some of our recent work has discussed the idea that change occurs most readily in the context of safety. We have also discussed the role of perceived risk in causing harmful anxiety in participants (Berman & Davis-Berman, 2005). Boot camps that utilize wilderness environments not only condone physical restraint and withholding of sustenance, they also sometimes "escort" children to their programs against the will of the participant. These escort services may charge up to $1,800 to take participants, sometimes out of their beds at night, into programs. Parents are asked to sign a waiver stating that they will not sue the escorts for "any injuries caused by 'reasonable restraint'" (Labi, 2004, p. 16). One of the ideas here is to keep the adolescent in a constant state of shock, not knowing what to expect. While many of our peers believe that escort services are necessary in certain situations, we believe that they are counterproductive to effective therapy.

As for the effectiveness of boot camps, a national survey of boot camps for adjudicated youth (MacKenzie et al., 2001) conducted in the mid-1990s found positive outcomes for boot camps on some key measures. When compared to traditional facilities for adjudicated youth (e.g., incarceration), the results for boot camps indicated that the youth in boot camps often reported positive responses to their environment. Similarly, boot camp staff had more positive attitudes about the wilderness setting than confined settings.

However, this survey also found that the anxiety level of boot camp residents was higher than for those in traditional settings. The boot camp residents felt that they were in more danger from staff than did participants in more traditional programs. Boot camps and traditional settings both were found to effect positive changes in anxiety and depression among residents.

Was this a valid comparison of boot camps and traditional forms of incarceration for adjudicated youth? This study was not as well controlled as researchers like to see, because the two groups of residents were not as comparable as a rigorously designed study would demand. The boot camps were more selective in that they admitted fewer youth who had psychological problems or were suicidal than did traditional settings. Also, many boot camp residents volunteered for the program, a reflection of higher motivation (MacKenzie et al., 2001). In a more recent review of studies that addressed the effects of boot camp experiences (Wilson, MacKenzie, & Mitchell, 2005), the authors were unable to find a significant difference between boot camps and more traditional settings on recidivism rates. At best, boot camps are controversial. A more negative view of boot camps is depicted by the National Mental Health Association (NMHA, 2004). In its compendium of best practices for treating youth in the juvenile justice system, the NMHA draws the following conclusions about boot camps for youth (pp. 17–18):

- Boot camps do not reduce recidivism.

- The confrontational approach used by boot camps is not appropriate for treating youth.

- Any positive gains shown in boot camps are likely to erode when youth return to the community.

- Boot camps have been unsuccessful in their attempts to rehabilitate participants.

- They cost more than community-based programs.

- They are not a quick fix.

This report concludes by saying: "The idea of shock incarceration as a tough, low-cost alternative to more intensive juvenile justice programming has not been borne out by more than 15 years of experience with boot camps across the country" (p. 18).

Szalavitz's book (2006) also presents research that shows these programs really aren't effective and includes actual cases of teens that participated in boot camp programs with less than favorable results. While her book is thought provoking and full of interesting background information, she raises some controversial points, which in our view are not supported either by the literature or psychological theory.

For example, she suggests that the problems with adolescents in this country today are exaggerated in order to sustain a profitable teen treatment movement. She asserts that most problems with teens are resolved without treatment or with minimal intervention by the early to mid-twenties. She then goes on to say that even if your teen's problems are more severe, they can usually be addressed through outpatient treatment. Again, she points to the programs themselves as trying to convince parents and professionals that teens need the more intensive and expensive residential treatment option. After raising these issues, she provides suggestions and help for parents in evaluating programs and in making decisions. Her ideas on adolescents clearly represent an extreme position. While we may not agree with her perspective on mental health disorders and treatment, we believe that her book is worth reading.

There is a great deal of information on boot camp programs on the Internet. As with wilderness therapy, there are sites with links to paid consultants who will refer customers to programs. One such company is Teen Options, which hosts a 24-hour hotline. On their website, they say that they are able to assess a personal situation and make recommendations and referrals to short-term or longer term programs for adolescents. A program run by this company (www.bootcampsforteens.com) presents itself as an unbiased referral source, but a read of the fine print on their website reveals otherwise. In fact, Boot Camp for Teens has a close relationship with Tipton Academy, and Tipton is a paid advertiser on the site. Boot Camp for Teens also acknowledges that it will generally recommend this program or another revenue-producing school or program if they deem it appropriate to do so. As with wilderness therapy educational consultants, it is wise to be wary of people who charge a fee to make referrals for adolescents, especially if these consultants have never personally met with the potential wilderness program participant or his/her family members.

A group from the University of South Florida has criticized this type of web-based marketing. In examining the recent increase in residential programs for children, they concluded that the American Psychological Association (APA) needs to become involved in providing parents with resources and advocating for both the examination and regulation of residential programs. Without this action, parents are left to rely on Internet marketing, which can direct them toward unregulated, unmonitored programs (Pinto, Friedman, & Epstein, 2005).

Promotional strategies sometimes include the publication of endorsements from parents of former boot camp participants saying that the program saved the life of their child. As a parent reading this type of statement, who wouldn't be convinced? But as Szalavitz points out, "No matter how powerful and plentiful individual accounts are, the plural of "anecdote" is not "scientific data" (Szalavitz, 2006, 13).

Recently, the U.S. Government Accountability Office (GAO)

undertook a comprehensive study of residential treatment programs serving youth. This investigation included programs in the United States and American-owned programs operating abroad between 1990 and 2007. Included in this study were wilderness therapy and boot camp programs (Government Accountability Office, 2007). Because many of the issues and concerns discussed from the Congressional testimony generated by this study involve risk management issues, we discuss the report in more detail in Chapter 5.

Making Good Choices

How do we make sense of all of this information and make good choices about treatment programs for adolescents? First, it is important to determine that the adolescent actually is in need of the intensive and expensive treatment that is offered by wilderness therapy programs. An adolescent should be evaluated by an unbiased physician and therapist to determine the appropriate level of care required. If the teen needs care outside of her/his home community, information gathering and research should begin. It is a good idea to start with programs that are monitored or accredited by a reputable organization (see Chapter 5 for information on this topic). Begin with research on the Internet, but be cautious, remember to beware of slick websites that make big promises.

Second, consumers need to be active, contacting the programs in which they are interested. It's difficult to ask questions and probe for information, but it is critical it be done. Questions should be asked about accreditation, regulation, staff qualifications, safety, and death and injury rates. Get to know the program's policies about escorting teenagers and about the use of restraint. We believe that programs that support coercion of any kind are suspect. Programs that appear to take any and all adolescents and will make admission decisions after a few minutes on the phone should not be considered.

Finally, if an adolescent needs a highly structured, strictly regulated program, we recommend a more traditional residential treatment center. Some of these residential programs expose participants to some wilderness experiences, so teens can benefit from time in the outdoors. This is in contrast to the punitive nature of boot camps.

Before we talk more about the specifics of individual programs, it is important to understand the basics of the theories and ideas that underlie wilderness therapy programming. In the next chapter, we explore some concepts and ideas that explain the power of this approach. Then, we present some traditional theories of change in language that is accessible to all.

References

www.aee.org

Berman, D., & Davis-Berman, J. (2005). Reconsidering posttraumatic stress. *Journal of Experiential Education, 28*(2), 97–105.

www.bootcampsforteens.com

Davis-Berman, J., & Berman, D. (1994). *Wilderness therapy: Foundations, theory and research.* Dubuque, IA: Kendall Hunt.

Government Accountability Office. (2007). Residential Treatment Programs: Concerns Regarding Abuse and Death in Certain Programs for Troubled Youth. Retrieved on October 10, 2007 from: www.gao.gov

www.coa.org

www.jointcommission.org

Jones, J. (2005). Wilderness therapy and the white hot glare of publicity. *Woodbury Reports,* Retrieved December 28, 2005, from http://www.strugglingteens.com

Kaplan, A. (2002). Wilderness programs for children: Benefits and risks. Retrieved January 5, 2006, from http://www.healthrising.com

Krakauer, J. (1995a). Loving Them to Death. *Outside,* October.

Krakauer, J.(1995b). Retrieved March 1, 2006 from http://outside.away.com/outside/magazine/1095/10f_deth.html

Labi, N. (2004) Want Your Kid to Disappear? Legal Affairs. Retrieved March 6, 2006 from http://www.legalaffairs.org

MacKenzie, D., Gover, A., Armstrong, G., & Mitchell, O. (2001). A national study comparing the environments of boot camps with traditional facilities for juvenile offenders. National Institute of Justice Research in Brief. Retrieved November 19, 2006, from http://www.ncjrs.org/pdffiles1/nij/187680.pdf

Maholland, K. (2005). Personal communication, August 25, 2005.

Mitten, D. (1999). Leadership for community building. In J. Miles & S. Priest (Eds.), *Adventure programming,* pp. 253–261. State College, PA: Venture Publishing.

National Mental Health Association (2004). *Mental health treatment for youth in the juvenile justice system: A compendium of promising practices.* Alexandria, VA: NMHA.

www.natsap.org

www.natwc.org

www.nzola.org.nz

www.obhic.com

www.outdoorcouncil.asn.au

Pinto, A., Friedman, R., & Epstein, M. (2005). Exploitation in the Name of "Specialty Schooling" What Counts as Sufficient Data? What are Psychologists to do? Retrieved February 20, 2006 from http://www.nospank,net.pinto.htm

Rogers, C. (1957). The necessary and sufficient conditions of therapeutic personality change. *Journal of Consulting and Clinical Psychology, 21,* 95–103.

www.strugglingteens.org

Szalavitz, M. (2006). *Help at any cost: How the troubled-teen industry cons parents and hurts kids.* New York: Riverhead Books.

www.twentytwenty.tv/

www.wilderdom.com/adventuretherapy.html

www.wilderness-therapy.org

Wilson, D., MacKenzie, D., & Mitchell, F. (2005). Effects of correctional boot camps in offending. Retrieved November 19, 2005, from http://www.aic.gov.au/campbellcj/reviews/titles.html

York, P., York, D., & Wachtel, T. (1982). *Toughlove*. New York: Doubleday.

CHAPTER 4
Anecdotes & Theories: The Transformative Power of Wilderness Therapy

discussion of theory is essential to developing a basic understanding of how and why wilderness therapy programs work, so the majority of this chapter will focus on theory. First, however, we present a handful of literature-based accounts of the process of change in wilderness therapy. Next, we turn to a presentation of some traditional psychological theories that have relevance to wilderness therapy. We discuss social learning theory, theories of self-esteem, transpersonal theories, systems theory, narrative therapy, and cognitive behavioral therapy. Although this may seem like a long list, we keep discussions short and encourage readers to further research theories of interest.

The chapter ends with a consideration of alternate models and concepts that are relevant to a theoretical understanding of wilderness therapy. These include "Mountains Speak for Themselves," perceived risk, a feminist perspective, and positive psychology.

Literary Accounts

Inspirational accounts of the healing aspects of the wilderness abound. Take, for example, the popular travelogues of Bill Bryson as he hiked the Appalachian Trail (Bryson, 1998) or the stories Peter Jenkins (2001) wrote about traveling with his dog in *A Walk Across America*. Stories like these give us a feeling of the magic that heals, realigns, and rebalances us when we leave civilization, live simply, and meet good-hearted folk along the trail. As compelling as these accounts can be, however, they fail to convey a complete understanding of what happens when we head into the wilderness, especially if our travels are meant to heal us.

Some accounts of wilderness travel attempt to portray the healing effects of wilderness without providing an adequate explanation of the mechanism of change. Les Blalock's book, *Meet My Psychiatrist*, is like that.

Blalock would have us believe, through beautiful photographs, that sitting on a park bench can cure homesickness, or that a log can substitute for a psychiatrist's couch. Oh, if only it were that simple.

For every story of rejuvenation and purification through wilderness journey, there is an account of the misery and tragedy that can occur in the wild. Take, for example, John Krakauer's *Into the Wild* (1996), which tells the true tale of Christopher McCandless, who hiked into the wilderness of central Alaska alone and with few possessions. The book explores the personal demons that took over McCandless' life and eventually led to his death. We cite this book because we've actually had people ask us if wilderness therapy experiences are similar to Krakauer's depiction of McCandless' solo adventure into an unforgiving, snow-covered wilderness. The answer is a resounding "no." The wilderness is no place for someone with serious behavioral or emotional problems to venture alone.

In general, writers who have chronicled the changes that take place in wilderness programs have taken two approaches. The first approach is to observe programs that apparently work and try to write about the changes that occurred. The second approach is more philosophical and abstract in that it looks at theories of behavioral and emotional change, with consideration of how these theories apply to wilderness therapy. In the following pages, we discuss three books: The first two fall into the first category and provide insight into what a wilderness therapy experience is like; the third falls into the second category, and reflects on the restorative power of nature.

Shouting at the Sky, by Gary Ferguson (1999), tells the story of a season during which Ferguson accompanied troubled youth on wilderness therapy treks in Utah (with a program called Aspen Achievement Academy). His account begins with the story of Ray, from Chicago, who wakes up one morning to find two men standing at the foot of his bed; they are there to escort him to Utah for a 60-day trek. He has a history of drug abuse, selling crack, and has been arrested for robbery. His behavior has all but destroyed his family.

Forced participation in this program is a last-ditch attempt by Ray's parents, who hope that their child will be like other "kids who didn't respond to conventional treatment getting better out there. No guarantees of course" (p. 6). As Ray's story unfolds, Ferguson describes the types of adolescents likely to be enrolled in this program for at-risk teens: Most don't want to be there, haven't been through therapy or rehab, but have had encounters with juvenile court and are looking at grim futures if not set on a new track. It's a compelling read and provides the reader an intimate feel for what the program entails and the resulting experiences of the

participants and staffers. But because Ferguson participated as an active observer rather than a researcher, his aim was to tell a story rather than document the catalysts of change. As such, he hints at and muses on the
subject, but doesn't get into the methodology that caused change. Was it
the closeness to nature? The immediacy of the consequences in nature? The
compassion of the leaders? Did it have to do with stripping the teens of
their worldly possessions and creature comforts? The use of metaphors?
Did group dynamics play a role? If you're looking for an absolute answer,
you won't get one. But if you seek to understand what it's like to participate
in one type of wilderness therapy program, *Shouting at the Sky* delivers.

   Crossing the Water (Robb, 2001) provides another first-hand account
of living in a therapeutic wilderness setting. This story is written by Daniel
Robb, a young man who goes to a small island off the coast of Massachusetts to teach eight boys who have been placed there by the Department
of Youth Services for approximately six months of treatment. Never having
worked with adjudicated youth, Robb isn't quite sure how to approach his
new charges. Not to worry, the program director tells him: "The best treatment we provide, I think, is a lack of therapy." Then he goes on to clarify
by saying, "By that I mean we don't get them to lie down on a couch and
rake through the shit of their childhood...." (pp. 32–33).

   In our opinion, the director's statement reveals a critical problem
with this program and others like it that reject traditional modes of treatment. Namely, it becomes the responsibility of those who are neither trained
as therapists nor educated about adolescent at-risk populations to effect
changes with the youth put in their charge. Thus, Robb is left to determine
how best to help the boys, because traditional therapy doesn't seem to be
the desired approach. Ironically, it is by reflecting on his own life, a process
denigrated by the director in the above quote, that Robb comes to the conclusion that the relationships the staff form with the residents and that the
residents form among themselves have the most curative power.

   Later in his tenure as a teacher on the island, Robb reflects on what
it takes to create change when he states: "I am beginning to see what much
of this teaching is about: sitting with the child ... time spent listening ..."
(p. 216). It sounds as though Robb is going beyond asking about the nature
of teaching. Is he really asking about the healing relationship and what it
takes to be a therapist? After considering the large percentage of residents
who return to their old lives and fall back into the criminal justice system,
the book ends with Robb raising the question, "Does the school work?" (p.
286). He believes it does and credits the caring and close relationships developed between staff and the kids for the success. Robb also acknowledges,

however, that there are no hard numbers that substantiate his conclusion, and that's because without a foundation in traditional mental health programming, among other things, the program isn't able to avail itself of the methodologies that allow psychologists and researchers to measure change.

Both of these first two books provide a sense of the promise that wilderness therapy holds for troubled youth who have struggled to benefit from more traditional sources of treatment. In our estimation, these books also expose the need for a synthesis between the frontline staff, who are often so close to the lives of participants, and the traditional fields of psychology, social work, and counseling.

In *The Experience of Nature* (1989), Kaplan and Kaplan explore how the wilderness restores people to a state in which they are more fully functioning. They argue that the restorative function of the natural environment can occur not only while on an extended wilderness trek, but also in one's own yard while, for example, working in a garden.

The Kaplans discuss how many of us feel emotionally "worn out, ready for a break or respite" (p. 178). This can happen as the result of stress, which they view as the anticipation of threat. Used in this way, the Kaplans' notion of stress is related to Selye's (1976) general adaptation syndrome, in which he described the reactions of organisms to prolonged stress. Stress can certainly tax an organism's system, to the point, as described by Selye, that it can lead to exhaustion (or even death). The Kaplans also point out that we can become worn out, not only by the anticipation of threat, but simply by prolonged work.

People often talk of the need to "get away from it all" when they are in such a state. When fatigued from stress or directed attention, escape may be better than staying in an emotionally draining situation. But escape alone is not enough, for if the new situation is confining, boring, or involves long periods where direct and focused attention is required, few benefits may accrue as a result of this experience. Environments that are restorative have a quality of "being in a whole other world." Kaplan and Kaplan (1989, p. 184) define this as:

> The sense of being in a whole other world implies extent—either
>
> physically or perceptually. To achieve the feeling of extent it is neces-
>
> sary to have interrelatedness of the immediately perceived elements, so
>
> that they constitute a portion of some larger whole. Thus there must
>
> be sufficient connectedness to make it possible to build a mental map
>
> and sufficient scope to make building the map worthwhile.

Two other elements are critical in order for an environment to be restorative, according to the Kaplans: There must be some element of interest or fascination, so that one is not bored and so that effortless, involuntary attention is used; and there needs to be compatibility between the environment and the individual. Without this compatibility, a person's abilities might not match environmental demands, resulting in the person having a hard time coping—hardly a scenario for renewal.

The outdoors, in general, and wilderness, specifically, provide the four essential components cited by the Kaplans as needed for restoration: Being in a natural environment involves getting away (escape), even if it means leaving one's office or home to walk in a park, although there is a clearer break from the everyday world when one participates in an activity such as canoeing down a remote river. With respect to the concept of extent, the wilderness can provide, on many levels, a feeling that one's immediate experiences are part of a larger whole. For example, while hiking a wilderness trail with a group, one may feel part of a like-minded community of adventurers. The trail feels part of a greater wilderness area, and hiking it provides a sense that one is mastering a set of skills that forms a body of knowledge. One might even begin to feel that there is continuity with other people who have traveled this same land in a similar fashion.

To those unfamiliar with wilderness, it can seem downright intimidating. But even if the environment is threatening or the activities involve risk-taking, the group-oriented nature of wilderness therapy programs can provide a feeling of compatibility, because everyone has a set of common goals (e.g., having fun, learning new skills, creating a supportive environment in which change is facilitated).

Moving from the Kaplans' ideas, we can conclude that the natural world provides limitless opportunities for growth and enjoyment, such as engaging in physical activity, pushing one's limits, enjoying or learning about flora and fauna, studying aspects of history, developing specific skills like orienteering, appreciating beautiful vistas, etc. Based on the wide variety of available experiences, we believe that programs should offer a range of possible modalities in order to enhance the compatibility between individuals and the environment. Browsing through an Outward Bound or National Outdoor Leadership School catalogue provides a thorough idea of the many forms of outdoors adventure that are available.

It is this variety of program types that makes theory difficult to apply and develop in the field of wilderness therapy. Keith Russell, a leading researcher in the field, has attempted to articulate a theory of program impact and program process. After studying four wilderness therapy programs, interviewing key staff, and even being a participant observer (2006), he was able to isolate factors that contribute to a model of impact and process, but also concluded that it is very difficult to discuss a theory of wilderness therapy impact or process. (For more about research done by Keith Russell and others, see Chapter 6.)

For greater insight into the dynamics underlying programming, it is instructive to look at traditional psychosocial theories.

An Overview of Theories

Learning about the theoretical underpinnings of a program can help parents in numerous ways: First, knowing something general about theory helps parents understand some of the language that programs use on their websites and other marketing materials. An understanding of theory also reveals information about the need for treatment, the kinds of treatments that might be expected, and even the reason a program operates the way it does. We include ideas from both traditional and less traditional theoretical perspectives

Traditional Theories

Social Learning Theory

Social learning theory suggests that learning occurs in a social context that involves observing others, weighing probabilities, and drawing conclusions about the causes and outcomes of events. For our purposes, we look at two components of social learning theory. First, consideration is given to Rotter's work on locus of control. Second, we discuss Bandura's theory of self-efficacy. Locus of control and self-efficacy can be understood as being part of the larger social learning theory.

Locus of Control. Julian Rotter formulated his ideas about social learning theory (1954) in a systematic way, with seven postulates and 12 corollaries. For our purposes, an abbreviated look at one aspect of his theory will suffice. One of the most often discussed changes participants experience as a result of wilderness therapy programs is an increased feeling of responsibility for the events in their lives. This relates to Rotter's notion of internal vs. external locus of control.

People who feel they are not responsible for the outcomes of their actions are described as having an external locus of control. Ideally, participation in wilderness therapy changes their locus of control so they come to believe that the outcome of their actions is a function of effort, skill, personality, or other internal factors (internal locus of control) rather than a function of fate, luck, or the power of others over them.

Rotter also talks about interpersonal trust and the role that trust plays in locus of control. Many of the participants of wilderness therapy programs lack trust, often for good reasons. When entering a new situation, such as a wilderness therapy program, there are few expectations because participants have little or no experience in this or related situations. As a result, one has to rely on trust and locus of control to determine whether or not a given behavior will be successful in the situation and will be rewarded or reinforced. It may be for this reason that participants new to wilderness programs are often tentative and overly cautious. As participants observe others, they may copy or model the behaviors of others. When others are behaving in successful ways and are being rewarded, this is called vicarious reinforcement. Watching others being rewarded can teach participants to engage in those positive behaviors themselves (Rotter, 1954; 1971).

As an example, consider the adolescent whose parents have told her numerous times to clean her room and to keep her personal items organized, all to no avail. From Rotter's perspective, she has not cleaned her room because either she does not believe that doing so will lead to positive reinforcement or that the rewards for cleaning her room are not desirable.

In base camp, wilderness leaders usually suggest that participants organize their belongings in their backpacks so that, for example, the rain poncho, toilet paper, snacks, and water are easily accessible. Reinforcement is immediate and direct the first time it rains, a participant has to go to the bathroom, needs a snack, or is thirsty. In this situation the participant quickly learns that only s/he controls the pack and that following the advice of the leaders reaps immediate rewards. This, in turn, might lead the participant to trust and model his/her leaders in order to experience an easier time on the trail. Finally, this increases the possibility that a participant leaves a program with a greater sense of interpersonal trust (because s/he feels s/he can rely on the word of the leaders) and locus of control (s/he controls much of what happens to him/her).

Self-Efficacy. Self-efficacy is a term used by Bandura (1977; 1982) to describe the belief that one can perform a given behavior. Self-efficacy differs from locus of control in that the former concerns the probability that one can successfully execute a behavior, and the latter pertains to the belief that a given behavior will result in a specific reinforcement or reward.

Our judgments of self-efficacy do not have to be accurate. Some people may believe they have the ability to accomplish something without actually being able to do it. Self-efficacy depends on four sources of information from which individuals judge their ability: (1) performance attainments,

(2) observing the performance of others, (3) verbal persuasion and other types of social influence, and (4) physiological states (Bandura, 1982). Of these four types of information, performance attainments are the most powerful because they involve actual attempts to master the environment. If one is successful, self-efficacy is enhanced. If a person tries to perform a behavior under at least moderately favorable circumstances and fails, however, feelings of self-efficacy are lowered. Self-efficacy can also be altered vicariously by observing others. In this way, one's own self-efficacy can be heightened or lessened by observing the efforts of others to whom we feel similar. For example, a participant's efficacy about being able to complete an activity may be influenced by watching another like-minded participant engage in the activity.

Verbal persuasion is the technique most used by therapists but may be of limited value. Bandura suggests that trying to convince someone to do something (persuasive efficacy) has the "greatest impact on people who have some reason to believe that they can produce effects through their actions" (1982, p. 127). That is, verbal persuasion may get people to try harder so that they succeed.

Low levels of self-efficacy can lead to feelings of depression and anxiety. This is related to the concept of learned helplessness (Seligman, 1975), in which an individual's behavior is found to be independent of the outcome of his/her actions. Bandura suggests the need to determine the source of the feelings of inefficacy. For example, does the person feel personally incapable (low self-efficacy judgment)? Or are his/her feelings of ineptitude a result of the environment being unresponsive or hostile to his/her efforts (what Bandura refers to as low outcome judgment)? Many of the adolescents with whom we have worked on wilderness therapy trips have a sense of helplessness that they attribute to their own inability but which is actually the result of an unsupportive, hostile, or abusive environment. Performance may also be hindered by focusing on what is unfamiliar or uncomfortable in a situation rather than on what is comfortable and within one's range of abilities. Bandura also mentions that self-efficacy can be undermined by being placed in an inferior role or being given negative labels.

Bandura's ideas suggest a combination of strategies for increasing self-efficacy. These strategies include learning a skill, observing others, verbal persuasion, or even altering cognitive assessments or interpretations of situations.

Another strategy is to alter the environment to make it more conducive to and supportive of change. In wilderness therapy programs, participants are given a variety of tools. Some are internal (e.g., learning how to ford a river) and others are external (e.g., wearing specialized hiking boots on the trail); some are solitary (e.g., writing feelings in a journal when one misses home) and others are collective (e.g., making a z-drag to get your kayak off a rock).

Theories of Self-Esteem

Ideas about *self* play a central role in modern personality theory that can be traced back 100 years to William James. Since that time, numerous theorists have included the notion of self in their theories, including psychoanalysts' use of the term *ego*. Since the Second World War, discussion about and understanding of the self has largely occurred through discussion of self-concept and self-esteem. Although these concepts are sometimes separated, they are often used interchangeably. While many theorists have discussed self-esteem and self-concept, two of the most notable theorists in this area are Abraham Maslow and Carl Rogers.

Self-Actualization. Abraham Maslow began his career in psychology studying the dominance behavior of monkeys. He noted that dominance was rarely based on physical aggression; rather, it was a resulting manifestation of an inner feeling. He later turned his focus to high-functioning people, while maintaining an interest in dominance and its origins. Maslow's definition of dominance parallels other theorists' ideas about self-esteem and self-worth in that he suggests that it arises from internal sources (Monte, 1980).

These insights led Maslow to study something he termed self-actualization (i.e., the inherent motivation to be fully functioning). That is, given a state of deprivation, more basic needs take precedence over higher needs, and only when a hierarchically lower need is relatively satisfied will a higher need emerge. The lower needs are also referred to as basic needs or deficiency needs. The most basic needs are physiological and are essential for survival. They include food, water, sleep, shelter from the elements, and a host of other needs. As such, they are satisfied primarily by external sources, as opposed to growth needs, which are satisfied from within. Maslow felt that it was not necessary to enumerate all of these needs (Goble, 1976). Once these needs are relatively sated, the need for safety emerges. Whereas a basic need may be for warmth, a safety need may be for comfort and security. These needs may also include the freedom from threat, a certain amount of orderliness and predictability, and the absence of pain and anxiety.

If these needs are met, the next needs to master are those for belongingness and love. Maslow's (1954) characterization of these needs could aptly be used to describe some of the needs of participants in wilderness therapy programs who have been severely abused. After a few days in the program, when physiological needs have been cared for and the routine of the program is established, a participant will begin to feel the need for higher types of fulfillment. As Goble (1976, p. 40) observed:

> [The participant] will hunger for affectionate relations with people in general, namely for a place in his group, and he will strive with great intensity to achieve this goal. He will want to attain such a place more than anything else in the world and maybe even forget that once, when he was hungry, he sneered at love as unreal or unnecessary or unimportant.

To this, and consistent with Maslow, we would add that our hypothetical participant "sneered at love" not only when he was hungry, but also, tired, hurt, scared, or in other ways deprived of his physiological or safety needs. When not deprived of these basic needs, people seek out affection and connectedness with others. This involves receiving care as well as giving it.

Esteem needs are next to emerge. Again, these needs emerge only when the more basic needs have been largely satisfied. Thus, Maslow theorizes that an individual will be concerned with an inner sense of value only when there are no threats to physiological and safety needs and when there is a sense of love and belongingness. Esteem needs take two forms, the first of which is for self-esteem. At this stage, people want to feel good about themselves because of a sense of mastery or achievement. This part of Maslow's theory meshes with other theories' concepts of self-esteem and is internal in its origin. The second form of esteem is more external and relates to feeling respect, recognition, appreciation, and even status.

The next need is the need for self-actualization. This is the need to achieve one's fullest potential, to become fully functioning, to grow to capacity in one's unique way. Maslow discussed this need as being the motivating force for growth in the personality and believed this force is easily thwarted. Thus, he believed that few individuals were self-actualized. Many of us, however, experience moments in which we are fully functioning. Maslow referred to these moments as peak experiences—moments when you become what you are doing, in which there is no sense of self-consciousness. Instead, you act spontaneously, expressively, and with a sense of freedom, control, and happiness.

Many people find that they are able to have peak experiences while hiking a trail. In such instances, they are not aware of the ground beneath their feet or the packs on their backs; instead, they are a part of the environment, moving with it, in harmony and bliss.

In what kind of environments can basic needs be satisfied? According to Maslow (1954), a variety of preconditions must exist. The environment must allow for people to express their feelings verbally or behaviorally (as long as no harm is done to others). People must also have the right to defend themselves against threat. There also must be fairness, honesty, justice, and orderliness. Goble (1976) mentions another aspect that is needed for growth to occur, one that captures the spirit of adventure pursuits, and that is challenge.

Self Theory. In consonance with Maslow, Rogers believes that people are motivated toward self-actualization. Their actions are directed by the desire for self-actualization, based on their own perceptions of their needs. According to Rogers (1959), the actualizing tendency begins in infancy as the baby differentiates experiences into those that occur in the outside world versus those that are internal. This internal awareness constitutes the formation of self-concept. As this self-concept develops, so does the infant's need for positive regard, a need that is universal. As an outgrowth of this need for positive regard, we develop a regard for ourselves (self-regard) that is learned in relationship to our experiences with others.

When we receive positive regard from others only when we think, feel, or act in certain ways, Rogers refers to this as conditional positive regard. In these circumstances, we learn that certain of our experiences lead to love and acceptance, while others do not. When that happens, some of our experiences become unacceptable. Acceptable experiences are not threatening to us and are perceived accurately. Unacceptable experiences threaten us because they have been associated with conditional regard and are distorted or denied from consciousness (the basic defense mechanisms). When this happens, a state of incongruence exists between self and experience. In other words, a psychic conflict grows between self and one's experiences (Rogers, 1959, p. 220).

This is in contrast with what happens when an infant grows up with unconditional positive regard. Then, the child's need for positive regard is satisfied regardless of what s/he experiences. There is no threat to his/her feelings of positive regard or self-image. All of the experiences are therefore equally acceptable and s/he is free to choose those experiences that lead to self-actualization and reject the others.

According to Rogers, those people who grow up with conditional positive regard sometimes behave in accord with their need for self-actualization (when their experiences are acceptable) and sometimes behave in response to the conditional positive regard they have received from others (when their experiences are unacceptable).

Therapy approached from this perspective aims to undo this process so that a person can accept all experiences and be true to his/her self regardless of the situation. This person is able to see reality clearly, with no need for denial or distortion. Therapy proceeds by increasing unconditional positive regard from significant others, which leads to an increase in the person's positive self-regard.

From Rogers' perspective, because participants in wilderness therapy programs have emotional conflicts and difficulties, they are in a state of incongruity with their experiences. Our role as wilderness therapists is to provide a warm, accepting environment, with group support in order to lessen feelings of personal threat so the person can lower defenses, leading to more congruence between the self and experiences. As a result, self-regard and adjustment should increase. From this theoretical perspective, this process allows the person to become more fully functioning.

Transpersonal Theories

Accounts of self-actualization and self-esteem have more recently been included in an area referred to as transpersonal psychology. In fact, Maslow was the first president of the Association for Transpersonal Psychology. This area of study aims to expand upon other movements in psychology.

In contrast to traditional theories, "Transpersonal approaches [go] beyond to see humans as intuitive, mystical, psychic, and spiritual. Above all, humans are viewed as unifiable, having the potential for harmonious and holistic development of all their potentials" (Hendricks & Weinhold, 1982, p. 8).

Tart (1975) defines transpersonal psychology as dealing with higher human processes that include spirituality and the development of human potential. Brown (1989) has approached outdoor adventure pursuits from the perspective of a transpersonal psychology practitioner. In attempting to account for personal growth that occurs in nature, Brown refers to increases in our sense of awe, inner calm, and other spiritual needs as a process of transformation. Brown advocates the use of specific techniques to enhance personal growth. These range from meditation and relaxation to the use of symbols and myths. The entirety of transpersonal psychology encompasses concepts from many of the Eastern religions and is beyond the scope of our theoretical concerns in this book. Our discussion is necessarily narrower and will focus on the use of symbols and myths.

Jung's conceptualization of the psyche is that it is comprised of three levels (for a more complete summary, see Hall & Nordby, 1973). The first, the consciousness, contains aspects of the mind of which the individual has direct awareness. The ego is that part of the consciousness that organizes one's experiences, memories, and feelings.

The second level of the mind for Jung is the personal unconscious. This area is the repository for those experiences that are not recognized as conscious, such as those that may have been conscious and were then forgotten. Or they may have been threatening to the person and were repressed or denied by way of defense mechanisms. These contents can become conscious when they are needed, making Jung's unconscious level similar to Freud's preconscious mind. The contents of the personal unconscious can cluster together to form complexes. Complexes can exert great force in terms of one's personality, as might be expected from someone who has a "guilt complex." This might happen when someone has repressed feelings of guilt that have not been dealt with, which as a result build up over time (Jung, 1954).

Complexes need not always be negative; in fact, they can be ruling passions. (Jung gives Van Gogh's passion for art as an example of a complex.) Jung speculated that complexes come from at least two sources. One relates to the traumas of childhood. For example, an abused child may grow up to make sure never to be vulnerable to others, could take up martial arts, become a spokesperson for the downtrodden, become a victim again, or even victimize others. A second source for a complex originates from a much deeper place in the psyche—from archetypes in the collective unconscious. According to Jung, the collective unconscious contains archetypes or prototypes of experience that are inherited as images from our ancestral past. They are not images, per se, but rather the predisposition to have certain experiences (Jung, 1975). In this way, we may find a campfire to be a source of security because our ancestors gathered around fires to ward off harm, provide warmth, and cook food. Campbell (1971) addresses the characteristics of archetypes: They are expressions of "common human needs, instincts, and potentials," and they are reflected in cultural traditions and myths.

Individuals who are psychologically unbalanced have fantasies and dreams that contain fragments of myths. These dreams are best interpreted by comparing them to myths that will allow the person to reestablish balance and direction. "The posture of the unconscious is compensatory to consciousness, and its productions, dreams, and fantasies, consequently, are not only corrective but also prospective, giving clues, if properly read, to those functions and archetypes of the psyche pressing, at the moment, for recognition" (Campbell, 1971, xxii–xxiii). In other words, the unconscious helps the conscious mind heal itself and understand the meaning of symbols and archetypes.

The mandala is an archetype that is commonly used in wilderness therapy programs. *Mandala*, a Sanskrit word for circle, refers to wholeness as reflected in circles. Mandalas represent the centering of one's personality. According to Jung, common mandalas are flowers and wheels—any round object that surrounds a central point. When we started our own program in 1985, we adopted the symbol of a wild flower, the trillium, within a circle. Although it was not designed with Jung in mind, its use as a healing symbol is certainly consistent with the mandala. Brown (1989) has participants in his program draw mandalas as a mechanism for positive change.

According to Jung (1975), therapeutic change occurs by helping the client unify polarized aspects of the psyche. The primary way of doing this is by getting in touch with the unconscious part of the psyche, then integrating it with the conscious part. Because archetypes reside in the unconscious, the use of symbols of transformation, like circles or four-sided symbols, aid in reaching the collective unconscious. In a wilderness therapy program, participants might be asked to form a circle, then begin to articulate, verbally or in writing, any experiences or relationships that they have had that could be symbolized by an unbroken circle. Group therapy sessions usually also take place in the circle formation. As participants sit in a circle in the middle of the woods, the symbolism of the unending and unbroken circle can be quite powerful.

Besides symbol creation, the other main strategy for creating change is through verbal means, such as in more traditional psychotherapy. Health is achieved when the two halves of the personality are balanced in such a way that the midpoint of the personality resides somewhere between the conscious and unconscious realms.

In a recent article, Willcocks (2004) discusses the integration of metaphors, symbols, and myths into experiential programs. One example she gives is that frontloading in an experiential program might include introducing the metaphor before the activity begins. Jung's ideas about complexes can also be used, and the complexes of the group itself can be examined. These are but a few of the ideas put forth by Willcocks as she attempts to integrate the Jungian perspective with experiential programs.

An example of the use of metaphors appears in *Shouting at the Sky* (Ferguson, 1999), mentioned earlier in this chapter, in which participants enter the program as mice and can become soaring eagles. Other applications within wilderness programs include holding group meetings in a circle around a fire, where inner changes can be discussed and then be transferred to life beyond by joining, as in a circle, a strong support system.

Systems Theory

A promising approach to working with troubled adolescents has been through the application of systems theory. According to this theory, adolescent problems occur within the family. While the family may or may not be responsible for the onset of problems (that is, some problems may be a function of biological processes or peer pressures), the family plays a role in maintaining, exacerbating, and alleviating problems. Some of the principles of systems theory as they apply to change within families include: (1) The family system in which the adolescent lives is an open system to the extent that exchange is possible with the outside environment (the larger system), but relatively closed to the extent that the family attempts to maintain its integrity in the midst of certain outside forces identified as "destructive"; (2) The family system attempts to maintain stability by dampening forces that would create instability; (3) In order for change to occur, there must be disequilibrium (instability); (4) When there are problems in the family, the problems must be experienced as dysfunctional before they can willingly be changed; otherwise, the family will attempt to resist change and maintain homeostasis (steady state); (5) Certain therapeutic situations make it easier for change to be made by families. These situations occur when the system is open and communication is free flowing. Importantly, some instability is needed for change to occur (Koman & Stechler, 1985).

Because of the interdependence of family members and the tendency of systems to maintain even what is at its core unhealthy stability, it is often difficult to change individual behavior without the assistance of the family system. That is one of the reasons that wilderness therapy programs can be so effective in creating personal change in adolescents: They provide a different system for the adolescent's behavior. That said, many problem behaviors are not consistent with wilderness therapy. For example, for the wilderness program to run smoothly, participants need to cooperate, communicate well, take responsibility for themselves and the group, etc. Individuals who are withdrawn, have trouble communicating, or are verbally aggressive often have trouble in wilderness therapy programs and quickly learn that their behavior is not rewarded.

Conceptually, wilderness programs can be seen as an alternative to the family, school, and community systems. Prosocial and more adaptive behaviors that were not directly reinforced in these other systems are reinforced in wilderness groups. Thus, it is often easier to change behaviors in the wilderness than it is at home. Of course, lessons learned and personal changes made in the wilderness program must be actively tied into the family and community in order create lasting change. It would be of little benefit to change behaviors in the wilderness if they could not be maintained when back in the community. Unfortunately, all too often the link between the wilderness program and the community is weak or nonexistent. Systems theory can also be used to conceptualize the planning and development of wilderness programs (Berman & Davis-Berman, 1991).

Narrative Therapy

Narrative approaches to therapy are based on the premise that our lives are a story, with a past, a present, and a future (Freedman & Combs, 1996). We are each the authors of our own story and the central characters of these stories (Berman & Davis-Berman, 1997; Davis-Berman & Berman, 1998). The role of the wilderness therapist is to help participants write their stories so that their present and future stories have a different ending than would have been predicted based on past stories.

In writing about narrative therapy in adventure settings, Allen-Newman and Fleming (2004) summarize the elements of this approach as a social process that involves a collaborative effort in which clients are the experts of their own lives. The therapeutic relationship from this perspective is seen as facilitating in the construction of a story that helps participants change, which can only occur when a person feels empowered, supported, and that s/he possesses a sense of efficacy.

An adolescent who is abusing drugs may not be able to envision him/herself going more than a day or two without using drugs. As the wilderness therapy trip progresses, that participant may begin to do well without drugs. This participant, with the help of the counselors and other adolescents, may begin to write a new life story, one that does not include drug use.

Cognitive Behavioral Therapy

Cognitive behavioral therapy (CBT) is based on the assumption that thoughts, feelings, and behaviors are all interrelated and that emotional distress and maladaptive behavior is related to faulty thinking. The relationship between CBT and wilderness therapy has been explored by Gillen (2003). In his article, he provides an in-depth description of CBT and suggests that it can be appropriately applied to adventure and wilderness therapy settings. He argues that CBT and wilderness therapy both focus on changing cognitions, are present and future focused, rely on a strong therapeutic relationship, and use stress to initiate change.

Beck (1976) believes that many behaviors are due to faulty beliefs. He encouraged clients to challenge their fears, confront their perceptions, and develop new beliefs about themselves.

Many times, wilderness therapy participants start the program afraid that they will fail the physical challenge of carrying a backpack for miles each day. During the trip, especially if lagging behind, the same participants will be challenged to confront the fear of failure and give the experience more of an effort. Often, as more effort is put forth, thoughts about failure change, improving both behavior and mood.

A more recent cognitive-behavioral theory has been presented by Seligman (1995), who proposes that optimism is learned and is a function of one's explanatory style. By that he means that how one explains success and failure is learned and influences feelings such as depression. Optimists take responsibility for their successes but attribute their failure to things beyond their control (e.g., luck, fate, powerful others), while pessimists take the opposite approach: They take responsibility for failure and externalize success (e.g., luck, fate, powerful others). Optimists and pessimists also have different views of permanence. Optimists believe that bad events are temporary, while pessimists believe they are permanent. Conversely, optimists see positive events as permanent while pessimists see them as temporary.

If a depressed wilderness therapy participant with a pessimistic outlook is given a compliment, s/he is likely to believe that the compliment is due to some external reason (e.g., "He is complimenting me only because he is a nice person and feels sorry for me"). S/he is also likely to see his success as temporary and specific to the situation in which it occurred.

The challenge of CBT is to retrain the mind's tendency toward negative or pessimistic thoughts and turn them into more positive or optimistic ones. In that wilderness experiences can involve many positive events, wilderness therapists have the opportunity to help participants note and change their pessimistic thoughts into more optimistic ones by internalizing success and viewing it as global and permanent.

See Figure 4.1 for a wrapup of important concepts from traditional theories.

▪ Locus of Control	▪ Family System
▪ Self-Efficacy	▪ Disequilibrium
▪ Self-Actualization	▪ Present and Future Stories
▪ Mandalas	▪ Learned Optimism

Figure 4.1 **Important concepts from traditional theories.**

Alternate Models

In addition to the more formal psychological and social theories that are often applied to wilderness therapy, there are many less formal, but widely used approaches to dealing with change in the wilderness. We talk briefly about "Mountains Speak for Themselves," ideas about perceived risk, a feminist perspective, and positive psychology.

Mountains Speak for Themselves

Bacon (1988) has written rather extensively about different models Outward Bound has used to develop and run its programs. He begins by discussing the notion of "Mountains Speak for Themselves." This approach was deemed to apply widely and could be used for all purposes, in wilderness settings with a variety of groups (Bacon, 1988).

The Mountain Speaks for Themselves philosophy is still in use today in some outdoor programs. It assumes that the outdoors is therapeutic in and of itself and that talking about or reflecting on outdoor experiences is unnecessary. In fact, adherents of this philosophy believe that to discuss therapy in the outdoors, or to even try to develop therapeutic methods, detracts from the ultimate power of the wilderness. Thus, participants grow and develop physically, spiritually, and socially, without needing verbal or therapeutic guidance (Bacon, 1988).

The Mountain Speaks for Themselves approach also assumes that the generalization of the participants' experiences on the trip to their everyday lives will naturally occur and that there is no real need to work on refining these skills or facilitating this generalization (Bacon, 1988).

These ideas are in contrast to the foundation beliefs of wilderness therapy programs where the focus is on therapy. The wilderness environment is seen as healing yet not sufficient alone to promote change.

Perceived Risk

A cornerstone of wilderness therapy has been to place participants in situations that are out of their comfort zones, which brings on a state of heightened arousal. This is believed to create a climate in which personal change is possible. Luckner and Nadler (1997) suggest that people learn and change when they are in a state of dynamic tension. This state is achieved when there is disequilibrium brought about by an internal conflict. The conflict occurs when there are challenges to a person's sense of safety and security. Thus, change is the result of a person's desire to alleviate a negative internal state and to return to a state of perceived safety and stability.

We should make the distinction between actual risk, in which case the individual has an elevated chance of physical injury, and perceived risk in which case the actual risk of injury is small but the participant feels as if there is substantial risk. The goal of all programs should be to keep actual risks low. Some wilderness therapy programs create a sense of perceived risk based on the notion that this is a critical element in the process of change.

We would assert that the field of outdoor education has often fostered a negative view of how change occurs. Traditionally, change in this field has been viewed as something that people are seen to do only when they are in conflict; otherwise, they resist change. In following the model of dynamic tension, change, as previously mentioned, occurs in a state of disequilibrium. This method of change is usually referred to as "taking someone out of their comfort zone" and constitutes an essential ingredient for change to occur. To cite an example of the need to create this negative state, consider the following quote from Luckner and Nadler (1997, p. 24):

> There are conditions or states that people can be placed in, in order to accentuate disequilibrium, dissonance, disorder, frustration, or anxiety. Enhancing these feelings increases the need to order, restructure, or alter one's cognitive map of the world and oneself in an effort to restore equilibrium.... Understanding these conditions and finding ways to create them can increase your ability to promote change.

In our opinion, the conditions they go on to mention are primarily, but not exclusively, negative. The negative conditions include effort (where "risk-taking is encouraged"), anxiety, perceived unpredictability, and perceived risk.

From a psychological perspective, this approach to creating change seems illogical. It is difficult to envision clients entering an office for counseling only to be told that they will be helped to reach their goals by increasing their anxiety, making them feel at risk, or sensing that they will be venturing into the unpredictable. In fact, it is usually the therapist's intent to create the opposite of these conditions. Thus, clients collaborate in a treatment plan so that the goals of treatment and the method for achieving these goals are explicit and very predictable. Counseling is intended to help people feel safe, minimizing perceived risk.

The danger in creating perceived risk, we believe, is that some participants may be pushed into a state of crisis under these circumstances. Thus, rather than facilitating change, a heightened state of perceived risk may actually interfere with a healthy process of change.

Consider, for example, a program that requires students to cross a narrow ledge many feet above a creek bed. Even if this activity has little chance of actual physical harm, it has the potential to bring on a crisis for those who do not have the inner resources to deal with such a challenge.

A test of this model was conducted by Leberman and Martin (2002), who asked Outward Bound students if the activities that pushed them out of their comfort zones were the same activities that they identified as leading to the most personal growth. They found that the activities that most often led people out of their comfort zones were physical in nature. However, those activities that led to the most growth-enhancing experiences were those that were social, creative, and reflective. These findings intuitively make sense for those familiar with traditional therapy, where it is the norm to foster a safe environment in order for change to occur. At a minimum, findings like these challenge the necessity of pushing people into a state of perceived risk as a necessary precursor for the instigation of change.

Boot camp programs, which rely on pushing participants beyond their limits, are examples of programs that capitalize on perceived risks. We feel that these approaches are not safe, as the difference between real and perceived risk depends on perspective. Risk is an individual experience, and we all have different definitions of what feels and seems risky. The simple act of being on a wilderness trip may feel like an extreme risk for some.

Feminist Perspective

Some have suggested that traditional models of wilderness education have historically been based on male-oriented conceptions of normative behavior and attitudes necessary for growth among groups (Mitten, 1999). Challenges to the traditional model of wilderness education have included the notion that its foundations are based on myths that serve as impediments for growth (Warren, 1999). These critiques have been referred to, by their authors, as being within the framework of feminist models (Mitten, 1994, 1996, 1999; Warren, 1996, 1999).

For our purposes, the importance of the feminist perspective is that it opens up the field of wilderness education and therapy to consider the needs of the participants in terms of how they learn and thrive. Such a model not only creates a better atmosphere for women but for other populations as well (Warren, 1999). It does so, for example, by emphasizing a nonhierarchical leadership structure, a model of leadership that utilizes the resources of the participants, and decision making that involves consensus (Warren, 1999).

Ideally, high-quality wilderness therapy programs function on the basis of groups and the relationships formed within them. The relationship and group process that leads to positive change has been referred to as a healthy trip community (Mitten, 1999). Mitten (1999, p. 255) has described some successful community themes that have the potential to lead to growth:

- Working with and within nature
- Enjoying nature for its own sake and not as a vehicle for risk taking or a proving ground for competency
- Flexible leadership that is constructive and safe
- An atmosphere of safety that is supportive of individual needs and differences
- Sharing and collaboration
- Focusing on strengths
- Respecting and valuing each person and their gifts
- Fostering individual goals and accomplishments

This model is significantly different in its outlook than those models that, for example, stress taking people out of their comfort zones in order to facilitate change. We agree with the feminist perspective that change is often best achieved when participants feel safe and secure. As we will see, this model bears some similarity to the positive psychology model discussed next.

Positive Psychology

Since World War II, when the field of clinical psychology came into its own, psychology largely has been problem focused. That is to say, psychology or at least the clinical application of psychology has looked for deficits in functioning in an attempt to help people reach a neutral state. In more concrete terms, psychologists have learned to diagnose and treat disorders rather than focus on psychological health. For example, a psychologist might diagnose and treat depression to help a person feel less of this negative emotional state.

That is not to say that psychology hasn't had the capacity to deal with positive states of being, and there are many examples of how it has—from the humanistic approaches of Maslow (1954), to studies of giftedness and marital happiness, to sports psychologists who try to help athletes optimize their performance. But positive psychology represents a relatively new movement in the field of psychology that has numerous implications for the field of wilderness therapy. Positive psychology has as its goal the fostering of excellence through the understanding and enhancement of factors that lead to growth. An analysis of positive psychology suggests that we can examine experience by studying positive individual traits, positive emotions, and prosocial attitudes (Seligman & Csikszentmihalyi, 2000). Individuals can have positive traits that include self-confidence, forgiveness, tolerance, creativity, passion for one's relationships and work, and perseverance. Subjectively, people can have positive emotional states of being that include hope, happiness, a sense of well-being, and contentment. Finally, a person can have prosocial attitudes that reflect characteristics that make for a better society, such as altruism, taking care of others, having tolerance, and being civil toward others.

What differentiates positive psychology from most other methods of psychology is that it attempts to help people go from a negative or neutral place to a positive one. Traditional methods focus more on psychopathology and negative functioning. Positive psychology helps people become more fully functioning in terms of their emotions, traits, behavior in groups, and perspectives on the future.

A prime example of positive psychology is the work of Mihaly and Isabella Csikszentmihalyi on the flow experience (Csikszentmihalyi & Csikszentmihalyi, 1999). Flow represents a state in which one experiences feelings of enjoyment, well-being, and competence while involved with and absorbed in an activity. Csikszentmihalyi & Csikszentmihalyi present six characteristics of the flow experience:

- The person has a specific goal in which the means and outcome are clear, where there is clear feedback, but the person's actions seem automatic and without pause to reflect on the event.

- There is a merging of action and awareness whereby the person has a sense of being in synch with the activity, seemingly without effort.

- There is a focus of attention on a limited stimulus field (attention is focused on a certain task).

- There is intense concentration in which one is so involved that s/he is not aware of him/herself, just the activity and his/her involvement with it.

- There is a sense of being in control of one's actions and the environment.

- Being engaged in the activity is so enjoyable and rewarding that the person wants to repeat the experience, which is so different than the mundane aspects of everyday life.
(pp. 1554–1556)

The Csikszentmihalyis' flow state is akin to Maslow's peak experience. In this state, people are fully functioning, have a clarity of purpose, and are lost in the activity. They are at one with what they are doing. However, an activity that leads to flow for one person is not predictive of what will lead to flow for someone else. Flow experiences are unique for each person.

It is hard to imagine that these conditions of flow could exist for someone who is experiencing disequilibrium, discomfort, or some of the other negative states that are associated with certain wilderness therapy programs as they create instability in the participants. It is our belief that wilderness therapy programs benefit from going beyond dealing with psychopathological deficits (although these might initially need to be addressed) to help participants achieve positive states of being. The positive psychology model, along with the feminist approach, have implications for leaders on wilderness therapy trips. (See Figure 4.2 for a list of some important concepts from these alternate models.) Both of these frameworks are completely contrary to approaches that are punitive, authoritative, or use coercion and physical punishment.

- Mountains Speak for Themselves
- Perceived Risk
- Healthy Trip Community
- Flow Experience

Figure 4.2 *Important concepts from alternate models.*

Summary

While anecdotal accounts might give us a sense of what occurs in wilderness therapy programs, they don't allow us to understand how change occurs or how to structure a wilderness therapy program so that it creates positive change.

More formal theories of psychological change provide the framework within which to understand the changes that can occur in wilderness therapy programs. Because each of the formal theories provides different components of understanding and change, none is complete alone. From our perspective, perceived risk as the motivation for change now seems outdated and may even be potentially dangerous for participants. The feminist perspective provides a framework for establishing the necessity for change, and positive psychology is an intriguing approach to focusing on strength, growth, and enhancement of abilities.

In the next chapter we continue to discuss risk and safety. We then review different levels of credentialing and regulation of programs and individuals in the field.

References

Allen-Newman, J., & Fleming, R. R. (2004). Making meaning of adventures: Narrative methods in adventure therapy. In S. Bandoroff and S. Newes (Eds.), *Coming of age: The evolving field of adventure therapy*, pp. 90–106. Boulder, CO: Association for Experiential Education.

Bacon, S. (1988). *Paradox and double binds in adventure-based education*. Eric Document Reproduction Service No. 296832, Greenwich, CT: Outward Bound, USA, 4–30.

Bandura, A. (1971). *Social learning theory*. Morristown, NJ: General Learning Press.

Bandura, A. (1977). Self-efficacy: Toward a unifying theory of behavioral change. *Psychological Review, 84*, 191–215.

Bandura, A. (1982). Self-efficacy mechanism in human agency. *American Psychologist, 31*, 122–147.

Beck, A. T. (1976). *Cognitive therapy and emotional disorders*. New York: International Universities Press.

Berman, D. & Davis-Berman, J. (1991). Wilderness therapy and adolescent mental health: Administrative and clinical issues. *Administration and Policy in Mental Health, 18*, 373–379.

Berman, D. & Davis-Berman, J. (1997). The essence of change is in the story. In R. Zabriskie and J. O'Connor (Eds.), The Bradford Papers (Vol. VII), 1-5. Bloomington: University of Indiana.

Blalock, L. (1977). *Meet my psychiatrist*. Bloomington, MN: Voyaguer Press.

Brown, M. (1989). Transpersonal psychology: Facilitating transformation in outdoor experiential education. *Journal of Experiential Education, 12*, 47–56.

Bryson, B. (1998). *A walk in the woods: Rediscovering America on the Appalachian Trail*. New York: Broadway Books.

Campbell, J. (Ed.). (1971). *The portable Jung*. New York: Penguin Books.

Csikszentmihalyi, M., & Csikszentmihalyi, I. (1999). Adventure and the flow experience. In J. Miles and S. Priest (Eds.). *Adventure programming*. (pp. 153–158). State College, PA: Venture Publishing.

Davis-Berman, J., & Berman, D. (1998). Lifestories: Processing experience throughout the lifespan. *Clinical Gerontologist, 19* (3), 3–12.

Ferguson, G. (1999). *Shouting at the sky: Troubled teens and the promise of the wild*. New York: St. Martin's Press.

Freedman, J., & Combs, G. (1996). *Narrative therapy: The social construction of preferred realities*. New York: W.W. Norton.

Gillen, M. (2003). Pathway to efficacy: Recognizing cognitive behavior therapy as an underlying theory of adventure therapy. *Journal of Adventure education and outdoor learning, 3,* 93–102.

Goble, F. (1976). *The third force.* New York: Pocket Books.

Hall, C. & Nordby, V. (1973). *A primer of Jungian psychology.* NY: Mentor.

Hendricks, G. & Weinhold, B. (1982). *Transpersonal approaches to counseling and psychotherapy.* Denver: Love Publishing.

Jenkins, P. (2001). *A walk across America.* New York: Harper Paperback.

Jung, C. (1975). *The archtypes and the collective unconscious.* London: Routledge and Kegan Paul.

Kaplan, R. & Kaplan, S. (1989). *The experience of nature: A psychological perspective.* Cambridge, England: Cambridge University.

Koman, S. & Stechler, G. (1985). Making the jump to systems. In M. Mirkin & S. Koman, (Eds.), *Handbook of adolescents and family therapy* (pp. 3–20). New York: Gardner.

Krakauer, J. (1996). *Into the wild.* New York: Anchor

Leberman, S. I. & Martin, A. J. (2002). Does pushing comfort zones produce peak learning experiences. *Australian Journal of Outdoor Education, 7,* 10–19.

Luckner, J. L. & Nadler, R. S. (1997). *Processing the experience: Strategies to enhance and generalize learning (2nd Ed.).* Dubuque, IA: Kendall/Hunt.

Maslow, A. (1954). *Motivation and personality.* New York: Harper and Row.

Maslow, A. (1962). *Toward a psychology of being.* New York: Van Nostrand.

Mitten, D. (1994). Ethical considerations in adventure therapy: A feminist critique. In E. Cole., E. Erdman, & E. Rothblum (Eds.). *Wilderness therapy for women: The power of adventure* (pp. 55–84). New York: Harrington Park Press.

Mitten, D. (1996). A philosophical basis for a women's outdoor adventure program. In K. Warren (Ed.), *Women's voices in experiential education.*(pp. 78–84). Dubuque, IA: Kendall/Hunt

Mitten, D. (1999). Leadership for community building. In J. Miles, & S. Priest (Eds.). *Adventure programming* (pp.253–261). State College, PA: Venture.

Monte, C. F. (1980). *Beneath the mask: An introduction to theories of personality.* New York: Holt, Rinehart and Winston.

Robb, D. (2007). *Crossing the water: Eighteen months on an island working with troubled boys—a teacher's memoir.* New York: Simon & Schuster.

Rogers, C. (1959). A theory of therapy, personality, and interpersonal relationships as developed in the client-centered framework. In S. Koch (Ed.), *Psychology: A study of a science* (Vol 3). New York: McGraw Hill. (Reprinted as "A theory of personality." In T. Millon, (Ed.), *Theories of psychopathology and personality* (pp. 217–230). Philadelphia: W. B. Saunders, 1973.)

Rotter, J. B. (1954). *Social learning and clinical psychology.* Englewood Cliffs, NJ: Prentice-Hall.

Rotter, J. B. (1971). Generalized expectancies of interpersonal trust. *American Psychologist, 26,* 443–452.

Russell, K. (2006). Brat camp, boot camp, or....? Exploring wilderness therapy program theory. *Journal of Adventure Education and Outdoor Learning, 6,* 51–68.

Seligman, M. (1975). *Helplessness: On depression, development, and death.* San Francisco: Freeman.

Seligman, M. P., & Csikszentmihalyi, M. (2000). Positive psychology: An introduction. *American Psychologist, 54*, 5–14.

Selye, H. (1976). *The stress of life.* New York: McGraw Hill.

Tart, C. (1975). *Transpersonal psychologies.* New York: Harper and Row.

Warren, K. (Ed.) (1996). *Women's voices in experiential education.* Dubuque, IA: Kendall/Hunt.

Warren, K. (1999). Women's outdoor adventures. In J. Miles, & S. Priest (Eds.). *Adventure programming* (pp. 389–393). State College, PA: Venture Publishing.

Willcocks, C. (2004). Integrating Jungian psychology into experiential programming. In S. Bandoroff and S. Newes (Eds.), *Coming of age: The evolving field of adventure therapy,* (pp. 73–89). Boulder, CO: Association for Experiential Education.

CHAPTER 5

Making Sense of Credentialing

Numerous organizations and associations regulate, license, accredit, and otherwise monitor wilderness therapy programs. While such monitoring doesn't guarantee safety, quality, or effectiveness, it is evidence of a program's commitment to mitigating risk by meeting standards based on best practices. In this chapter, we discuss state regulation, professional membership organizations, and accreditation as ways that programs may pursue to enhance their programming and credibility. We also address credentialing of individuals, both in the U.S. and abroad. In order to avoid overusing industry jargon, we use the term credentialing when referring to certification, registration, and licensing, even though they represent three unique types of program monitoring systems.

Before we begin, we must say that we strongly support credentialing of both individuals and programs. However, our perspective is not shared by all. One of the arguments against credentialing is that credentials can't actually deliver on what they promise, because on-site evaluations are one-time analyses of a fluid system in which numerous variables are constantly changing (i.e., staff, environment). Another is that outside rules may hamper a program's creativity. And yet another argument involves cost: Going through a credentialing process and maintaining credentials costs significant amounts of money—costs that often are passed along to the patients in the form of increased fees.

The Significance of Credentials

Wilderness therapy, by nature, carries some inherent risks. First there is the issue of environment: Simply spending extended periods of time in unfamiliar environments like the wilderness raises the risk of injury or incident. In addition, wilderness therapy programs often expose youth to activities such as kayaking, climbing, backpacking, and skiing. Obviously, participating in these activities is riskier than sitting in a therapist's office. Although the safety of participants can never be completely guaranteed, wilderness therapy programs that subject themselves to official assessments by external credentialing bodies demonstrate a commitment to operating as safely and effectively as possible. Different types of regulatory measures, including state regulation, membership criteria, and standards-based accreditation are discussed later in this chapter.

The Risk Factor: Statistically Speaking

The leading research on the safety of wilderness therapy programs (Cooley, 2000; Russell & Harper, 2006) has been done by the Outdoor Behavioral Healthcare Research Cooperative (OBHRC). When Cooley looked at the statistical probability of injury in a number of sports and in four Outdoor Behavioral Healthcare Industry Council (OBHIC) programs, he found that a high-school football player or cheerleader was 18 times more likely to suffer an injury than was a participant in one of the four programs he assessed. Other comparisons showed that the risk of injury in the four wilderness therapy programs studied was similar to that for cross-country skiing and less than canoeing or participating in a summer adventure camp. Also, Cooley's study showed that in a 50-day program with seven adolescents, odds were that there would be one injury, one illness, and one evacuation every third 50-day trip. The wilderness therapy injury rate of 1.12 per 1,000 field days found by Cooley's study is similar to the injury rates for adventure programs (1.29 per 1,000 field days) (Leemon, 2006).

Russell and Harper (2006) looked at incident data for the 10 wilderness therapy programs that belonged to OBHIC from 2001 through 2004. Incident data refers to: holds and restraints, runaways, illnesses and injuries that take the participant out of programming for more than 12 hours, and fatalities. In this study, incidences were computed in two ways: incidences per 1,000 participants and per field days, where a field day was one 24-hour period in the field for one participant. Their data for 2004 found: 1.5 holds (physically assisting a participant by, for example, holding on to an arm); 0.38 restraints (physically immobilizing a participant) per 1,000 participant field days; 1 of every 98 participants tried to run away; 1 of every 55 participants had an injury that took him/her out of program for 12 or more hours; and one death per 1 million participant field days.

Both studies included only OBHIC-member programs, so the findings do not reflect the inherent risk of all wilderness therapy programs—just those that have met OBHIC's membership criteria (for more about that criteria, see page 75). While other programs might be just as safe, corresponding data is not as readily available. This data also does not account for programs that are unregulated and that don't collect data on safety. Although it is impossible to accurately count the number of these programs, a significant number do exist (Szalavitz, 2006).

On the opposite end of the research spectrum are the findings provided in testimony on October 10, 2007, by the Government Accountability Office (GAO) to the U.S. House of Representatives. Its study focused on allegations of abuse and death in programs for at-risk youth occurring between 1990 and 2007 (GAO, 2007). The study on which the GAO's findings were based used the following framework: It interviewed experts, reviewed articles in print and on the Internet, gathered information from the National Child Abuse and Neglect Data System, and reviewed legal cases. The GAO found thousands of cases of alleged abuse in residential programs for youth, some of which resulted in the death of residents. Its study looked into 10 cases involving the death of adolescents in residential programs, and found that ineffective management, untrained staff, inadequate nourishment for residents, negligent operating practices, and inadequate equipment were to blame.

Responses to the GAO testimony have been varied. News articles, like one that appeared in the *Washington Post* (Schneider, 2007), have tied deaths in boot camps and residential treatment centers to wilderness therapy. In an attack on the congressman who initiated the request for the GAO study, Woodbury (2007) accuses Congressman Miller of using the GAO to create "legislative drama ... in his bid for Congressional fame." Perhaps of most interest to professionals within the field are the messages on the adventure therapy listserv, whose subscribers are primarily members of the Therapeutic Adventure Professional Group of AEE. For the most part, these messages have called for those in the adventure therapy field to use this report in a nondefensive way to examine our practices; to continue to distinguish between quality, certified programs and those that operate according to their own set of rules; to conduct and disseminate the results of research that points to the effectiveness of wilderness therapy; and to continue to look at defining standards for wilderness therapy. Those interested in tapping into the dialogue occurring on this listserv can subscribe by going to the www.listserv.uga.edu and registering for ADVTHE-L listserv. Of interest are the messages in the October 2007 archives.

While the GAO report made some valid points about the risks and types of problems that plague some programs, like hiring untrained staff, the study's shortcomings are significant, starting with its methodology. It was not able to get an accurate count on the number of alleged cases of abuse and could not determine the number of cases in which there is proof of neglect. Further, it did not differentiate between different types of programs, and instead lumped all residential treatment programs together. And it paid no regard to the effectiveness of wilderness therapy. This is not to say that the GAO study should be disregarded. In our opinion, by highlighting worst-case scenarios, it demands us to scrutinize what kind of regulation is required. If we are to benefit from this study, it will require sorting out the kinds of risks (and benefits) that are associated with specific factors such as: types of programs, the need for certification, state licensing, and accrediting bodies (or lack of), the amount of staff training needed, and more. It is only by delving into all the confounding variables in the GAO study that parents and therapists will be able to make informed decisions about programs, weighing the risks and benefits of a program for a given troubled adolescent.

Beyond the Physical Realm

In addition to physical safety, there are the issues of emotional and psychological safety to consider. Much has been written about the effects of stress, heightened arousal, and coping in wilderness programming, as well as the dangers of pushing participants too far out of their emotional comfort zones (Mitten, 1999). This perspective holds that people in psychological treatment are most likely to change when there is a state of emotional safety. While we concur with the above perspective and have written extensively on the subject (Berman & Davis-Berman, 2001, 2002; Davis-Berman & Berman, 2002; Berman, Davis-Berman, & Gillen, 1998), there are those who develop and administer wilderness therapy programs who believe that pushing participants out of their comfort zones is necessary in order to facilitate change (Luckner & Nadler, 1997). The point of view with which we align is based on the belief that when people feel threatened, they tend to close up, act defensively, and resist change. That is not to say that extreme stress doesn't foster change in many people (take, for example, the life-altering changes people make after undergoing serious, life-threatening medical or physical challenges). However, we do not believe that mental health professionals should subject those in their care to undue stress. Rather, it is our belief that responsible therapists create an atmosphere of safety and trust, as these are the underpinnings of the therapeutic relationship. These ideas are supported by some of the classic practitioners in the field of psychology in their writings on the process of therapeutic change (Maslow, 1954; Rogers, 1951).

Many wilderness therapy programs partner with "escort" services, which for a fee, send an adult into the home to physically escort participants to wilderness therapy programs. In our opinion, parents should carefully examine escort-service policies. Some programs encourage parents to misrepresent the journey to the wilderness therapy program as a family vacation. Then, when the family car pulls into the program parking lot, the participant is strong-armed from the car and brought into the program headquarters to begin the wilderness therapy experience. In our view, safety and coercion do not go well together; neither do trust and duplicity. Other people, however, believe that there are certain circumstances under which there is no other alternative.

Regulation, Licensing, & Accreditation

In order to further explore issues of risk management in wilderness therapy programs, we turn to a discussion of strategies that are used to assess programs with the intention of rendering them more safe and credible. We begin with an overview of state regulation, then turn to professional membership and accrediting organizations, and finally to the credentialing of individuals.

State Regulation

Many programs are accredited or regulated by the state in which they operate. Different states have different regulatory bodies for such programs, and some states have no regulatory programs at all. This inconsistency is currently the subject of the Government Accountability Office audit referenced earlier in this chapter. In some states, the Department of Child Services regulates wilderness therapy programs; in other states, such regulation falls under the domain of the Department of Human Services. The following states currently regulate wilderness therapy programs:

- Alabama
- Georgia
- Idaho
- Louisiana
- Nevada
- New Jersey
- Oregon
- Texas
- Utah
- Virginia

Because there are as many varieties of state regulation and licensure as there are states, we have chosen to provide an overview of Oregon's rules (Oregon Administrative Rules ORS: 413-210-0800) as an example of state regulation, because they are fairly comprehensive and provide an example of carefully developed legislation. Also, the rules for Utah (Utah Administrative Code R501-8.) and Nevada (Nevada Revised Statutes Chapter 432A), where many leading programs are administered, are similar to those of Oregon. Nevada, Utah, and Oregon have regulations that govern outdoor youth programs and are licensed through each state's Department of Human Services. Utah's rules were recently revised (October 1, 2007) and contain more restrictive language and penalties that can include immediate revocation of a program's license for noncompliance with the rules (UT Administrative Code R50 1-8-23).

In some states, wilderness therapy programs fall under the category of Outdoor Youth Programs. Oregon defines Outdoor Youth Programs in the following way:

> A program that provides, in an outdoor living setting, services to
> youth who are enrolled in the program because they have behavioral problems, mental health problems, or problems with abuse of
> alcohol or drugs. (ORS 413-210-0809)

Programs that fall under these statutes in Oregon must be licensed by the state, open themselves up for inspection, and keep extensive files regarding staff and patients. Adolescents in these programs must be under the care of a multidisciplinary team that includes medical personnel (physician, physician's assistant, or nurse practitioner), a mental health professional (licensed psychologist, social worker, or counselor), and a substance abuse professional (ORS 413-210-0809).

Admissions screenings must be completed by an experienced staff person, with attention to social and health background information, a psychosocial assessment, and mental health and substance abuse assessments. It is notable that in Oregon there are no requirements for the staff person conducting the mental health assessments to be a licensed mental health professional, although the multidisciplinary team is required to view the admission if there are questions about the appropriateness of the admission. There is also no requirement that the applicant be evaluated in a face-to-face assessment by a licensed mental health professional at the outdoor youth program or in the applicant's hometown. It is therefore entirely possible that an adolescent can be admitted to a program solely on the basis of phone interviews with an admissions counselor and written material submitted by parents.

As such, an adolescent's first contact with outdoor youth program staff can be after admission to the program. Before leaving on a wilderness trek, Oregon statutes require that staff interview new participants and provide them with an orientation. Medical staff must review the adolescent's health history and perform a physical exam. Once in the field, the participants must have individual service plans prepared by clinical staff that are periodically reviewed and updated.

Because the quality of a program often lies in the quality of its staff, it is worthwhile to consider the Oregon minimum criteria for staff qualifications.

- Executive directors must be at least 25; have five years of employment in social service or wilderness fields, at least one of which is administrative, and have relevant knowledge and experience in order to run a program.

- Field directors must be at least 25; have one year of experience as an outdoor youth program staff or a year of college in recreation therapy or a related field; hold a Wilderness First Responder (WFR) certification; and have completed a nonviolent crisis intervention course.

- Senior field staff must be at least 21; have a year of college or a year of experience in recreation and adventure activities; have 40 days of field experience; hold a WFR; and have completed a nonviolent crisis intervention course.

- Field staff must be at least 21; have a high school diploma; and have CPR and first-aid training.

In addition, all staff must undergo specific staff training regarding issues such as Leave No Trace, ration planning, safety, and other relevant topics as specified in the statutes. In the field, there must be at least 2 staff per 6 participants. If there are female participants, there must be a female staff. One of the female staff must have Senior Staff status (ORS 413-210-0809).

Almost 40 percent of the remainder of the Oregon outdoor youth program statutes address risk management issues. Included in these statutes are rules about storage and administration of medication, transportation, solo experiences, emergencies, physical activity limits, critical incidents, health care, behavior management, food and water requirements, clothing and supplies.

As this overview of Oregon's rules shows, they aim to protect adolescents and ensure that they receive qualified care. They do so by requiring certain standards be met and by prohibiting specific practices. However, while they do cover the basics, they fall short of mandating high levels of treatment. Specifically, even though field staff spend the most time with adolescents deemed to be in need of mental health or substance abuse treatment, they are not required to have more than one year of college. This is a far cry from the requirements of professionals who treat adolescents in community settings, such as hospitals or clinics, where minimum degree and licensure requirements exist. Outdoor youth programs can hire staff with more credentials than those specified by Oregon's administrative rules, but the fact that a program is licensed does not guarantee that staff possesses credentials greater than those required by the minimum standards.

Although Oregon's rules promote safety in some ways, we think that these credentialing requirements fall short of what ideally constitutes best practice. These state regulations, however, are in line with others and are even more well-written than many. However, just because a wilderness therapy program is state licensed and regulated, don't assume that the same level of staff education and expertise exists as compared to a more traditional, community-based program.

Professional Membership Organizations

Because state licensing is not enough to guarantee a safe or therapeutic experience for a troubled adolescent, it is wise to inquire about a program's affiliation with any of the numerous professional organizations that assess the quality of wilderness therapy programs. There are three major professional organizations that specifically relate to wilderness therapy programs. These include the Outdoor Behavioral Healthcare Industry Council (OBHIC), the National Association of Therapeutic Wilderness Camps (NATWC,) and the National Association of Therapeutic Schools and Programs (NATSAP).

Outdoor Behavioral Healthcare Industry Council

In the late 1990s, a group of organizations providing wilderness therapy services to adolescents formed a professional membership organization called the Outdoor Behavioral Healthcare Industry Council (OBHIC). Part of OBHIC's mission is to set the standard by which families can choose wilderness therapy programs for their children. Its purpose is to promote high standards of care in programs and serve as leaders in the field of wilderness treatment. This organization accepts only wilderness programs that consider themselves to be behavioral health care programs as members.

While OBHIC does not put member applicants through a standards-based review process, its membership criteria are fairly stringent. For example, if a program wants to become a member of OBHIC, its first year is provisional. The application for membership must be reviewed and approved by the Membership Committee of OBHIC and must include letters of recommendation from a professional referral source, a past participant in the program, and a family member of a past participant. Importantly, all programs seeking membership must be licensed, certified, or recognized by agencies that are deemed acceptable to OBHIC (www.obhic.com).

OBHIC is an active organization that includes a number of working committees, such as: a standards and quality committee, a research committee, a government relations committee, and a land use committee, among others. It also publishes a set of philosophical and ethical standards by which member programs are expected to abide. OBHIC currently has 15 program members, primarily located in the western United States. They meet on a regular basis, share data on research done on member programs, and establish guidelines for the organization's member programs. (See Figure 5.1 at the end of this chapter for more about the commission's guiding principals.)

In 1999, OBHIC made a research connection with the University of Idaho's Wilderness Research Center. The aim of the initiative, named the Outdoor Behavioral Healthcare Research Cooperative (OBHRC), was to advance the field through research-based study. The initial tasks of this research group involved defining outdoor behavioral health care and developing and supporting a national research project that examined the process and effectiveness of wilderness therapy programs. Currently, this group is under the direction of Dr. Keith Russell at the University of Minnesota. As mentioned earlier in this chapter and discussed at length in Chapter 6, this research group has generated some of the most important data on the process and outcome of wilderness therapy programs.

Headquarters: Oregon
Website: www.obhic.com
Phone: 541-926-7252, ext. 202

National Association of Therapeutic Wilderness Camps

NATWC is committed to serving as a resource for families in choosing wilderness programs. Established in the mid-1990s after a death in a wilderness therapy program, its mission statement in part reads: "We support the establishment and continuation of therapeutic wilderness camping organizations with the attendant responsibility to educate the public as to the existence of such organizations and their success in helping troubled young people change their lives for the better" (www.natwc.org).

NATWC's more than 50 members include wilderness therapy

programs that serve youth, as well as more residentially based wilderness camps. While admission to NATWC doesn't involve a probationary period, applicants must document that they are licensed or accredited if that is required in the state in which they operate. (See Figure 5.1 at the end of this chapter about the association's guiding principals.)

In alignment with its founding principals and mission statement, NATWC has been especially outspoken about issues regarding risk management. Its members are committed to separating themselves from boot camps and from the programs in which deaths have occurred. NATWC has developed a set of ethical principles that includes the right of all participants to opt out of activities, strongly supporting the ideology that participants should not be forced or coerced in any way to engage in any activities. They also support prohibiting restraint as punishment and only using restraint as a last resort. Finally, they support programs in providing adequate food, water, shelter, and staff training.

NATWC hosts an annual national conference and publishes the *Journal of Therapeutic Wilderness Camping*. NATWC has also developed three levels of certification for wilderness counselors: Wilderness Counselor, Master Wilderness Counselor, and Senior Wilderness Counselor. NATWC doesn't actually offer the courses that are needed to earn the various certificates; rather, it serves as an evaluative organization, and applicants interested in earning one of the above designations must demonstrate that they have met certain requirements as determined by NATWC for each level of certification. The applicant's skills also must be certified by a peer review. This documentation is submitted for evaluation by NATWC through the program at which the applicant is employed.

Headquarters: Pennsylvania
Website: www.natwc.org
Phone: 724-329-1098

National Association of Therapeutic Schools and Programs

NATSAP was founded to serve as a national resource for programs and professionals that serve youth with emotional and/or behavioral problems. (See Figure 5.1 at the end of this chapter for more about the association's guiding principals.) NATSAP is committed to supporting and encouraging the provision of high-quality services to young people in all types of treatment settings. As such, its members include traditional residential care and boarding schools, as well as wilderness programs.

Because providing information on ethics and practice is central to NATSAP, it has developed a set ethical principles and standards for good practice. These guidelines (and its member directory) are listed on its website and are also available in hard copy. NATSAP serves as a resource to professionals and families as they consider therapeutic programs. NATSAP also sponsors an annual national conference and annual regional conferences, and publishes the *Journal of Therapeutic Schools and Programs*.

NATSAP's membership process requires that members have been in operation for at least 2 years, but newer programs can be given associate or provisional membership status. All member programs must be licensed by their state agency or accredited by a mental health accreditation agency. They must provide services that are overseen by an independently state-licensed clinician. Of the three professional organizations discussed here, NATSAP is the only one to hire lobbyists and has taken a lead role in representing the field in Congress regarding the GAO investigation into residential treatment programs.

At this time, more than 100 programs are members of NATSAP, including 29 wilderness programs and 14 outdoor therapeutic programs, with some programs appearing on both lists.

Headquarters: Arizona

Website: www.natsap.org

Phone: 928-443-9505

Accreditation & Accrediting Bodies

Some programs are state regulated and are members of the major professional associations in the field. Others want to go even a step further and pursue accreditation. While state regulations often require strict adherence to guidelines for staff and participants, professional organizations do not have such a rigid set of rules. Accrediting bodies require that programs conform to a set of published, standards-based requirements. Achieving accreditation is a lengthy, involved process that involves performing a detailed self-study, as well as site visits by trained accrediting-body reviewers, and ongoing monitoring.

Three major organizations in the United States accredit outdoor programs: The Association for Experiential Education, the Council on Accreditation, and The Joint Commission. As we did with the professional organizations, we discuss each of these organizations, providing information about their mission, services, prominence in the field, and contact information.

Association for Experiential Education

Even though the Association for Experiential Education (AEE) is a ofessional membership association like those profiled in the previous section, we have included it in this section because AEE has a well-developed accreditation program and has been a leader in accrediting outdoor programs since 1994. First, a bit about the association as a whole: The AEE serves more than 1,400 members worldwide. Its membership consists of individuals as well as programs. AEE offers six levels of membership, all of which receive different services and, accordingly, pay different dues. Because AEE is first and foremost a membership association, anyone can join by paying fees.

In an effort to meet the needs of its diverse membership, AEE has five special interest groups (called Professional Affiliation Groups), one of which is the Therapeutic Adventure Professional Group (TAPG). Many professionals who work with youth in wilderness therapy programs are members of this professional group, and the TAPG hosts a biannual conference where members come together to share best practices and research.

AEE hosts an annual international conference and eight regional conferences and publishes a scholarly peer-reviewed journal called the *Journal of Experiential Education.* It also provides resources and professional development opportunities to professionals in the many fields related to experiential education and serves as a major accrediting organization of outdoor programs. (See Figure 5.1 at the end of this chapter for more about the association's guiding principals.)

The Association for Experiential Education has distinguished itself in the area of program accreditation and, at this time, it is one of the major accrediting bodies for therapeutic wilderness and wilderness programs in the United States. AEE's accredited members (of which there were 48 at the time of publication) have undergone a standards-based evaluation process in order to attain accredited status. The accreditation process takes approximately 18 months and begins with a self-study, followed by an on-site review (of programming, as well as such things as manuals, permits, inspections) and a written review. Programs that achieve AEE accredited status can be confident that they meet or exceed recognized industry standards, as outlined in the fourth edition of the *Manual of Accreditation Standards for Adventure Programs* (Leemon, Pace, Ajango, & Wood, 2005). The AEE accreditation standards, because they apply to all types of experiential programs, do not address therapy in particular but explicitly focus on all general aspects of adventure program operations. Overarching topics covered during the accreditation process include: program philosophy and goals, and educational and ethical principles; program governance, operations, and oversight; and technical skills (both land and water based). The 44 subsections that fall under those larger groupings range from equipment to international considerations, transportation to hygiene, and hiking to SCUBA diving. Every subsection contains up to 20 standards, and programs seeking accreditation must document how they comply with each of the standards that apply to the programming they provide. It's an in-depth process that through its self-study process helps programs take a hard look at how they do what they do, and through the review process promotes professionalism, proper operations, risk management practices, and effectiveness.

Programs that achieve AEE accredited status must comply with extensive criteria. The manual points out numerous benefits of going through the accreditation process, including: "Programs that go through the accreditation process have found [it] very educational and beneficial, and most claim that their risk management systems have been improved greatly as a result." The authors go on to point out that, " ... accreditation is not a guarantee that clients or staff of accredited programs will be free from harm" (Leemon, Pace, Ajango, & Wood, 2005, p. 10). Obviously, no program can make hard and fast guarantees about safety or effectiveness, but this type of stringent accreditation process goes a long way toward inspiring confidence in a program.

The Accreditation Council for AEE approved standards for therapeutic adventure programs at the 2007 International AEE Conference (H. Wood, personal communication, November 12, 2007). When completed, they will be added to the existing accreditation manual (Leemon, Pace, Ajango, & Wood, 2005). Some of the proposed changes that apply to therapeutic adventure modify existing standards. For example, changes to existing standards call for staff to be appropriately trained to work with the specific populations, under proper supervision, and in accord with applicable state and federal laws.

Other changes to the manual will include new wilderness therapy–specific standards. These updates require programs to have written policies and procedures for conducting therapeutic activities, with a specific, appropriate curriculum for the population. New safeguards for participants require adequate instruction with briefings that frame the activity to minimize risk and to enhance the experience, with proper supervision and at a pace that prevents injuries.

Special considerations are also being added for high-risk concerns. Included among these are written policies and procedures concerning the dispensation of medications to participants, the use of restraints and holds, and protocol for managing psychiatric emergencies.

Headquarters: Colorado
Website: www.aee.org
Phone: 303-440-8844

Council on Accreditation

The Council on Accreditation (COA) accredits more than 1,500 behavioral health care and social service organizations in the United States and Canada. In the early 1990s, we were part of the original panel that drafted its standards for the accreditation of wilderness therapy programs. Since that time, extensive revision of the standards has occurred, resulting in the current 8th edition of the COA standards (Council on Accreditation, 2007). COA accredits nearly three dozen types of services, including wilderness therapy, ranging from crisis hotlines, domestic violence services, debt counseling, refugee resettlement, vocational rehabilitation, outpatient mental health, adoption, child protective services, and residential treatment. (See Figure 5.1 at the end of this chapter for more about the council's guiding principals.) This organization is large and complex, and its accreditation process, which involves self-study, site visits, and continued monitoring, is highly regarded.

The COA standards define wilderness and adventure-based therapeutic outdoor services as offering "an intensive therapeutic experience based on outdoor, educational, clinical, and other activities that involve physical and psychological challenges" (Council on Accreditation, 2007). The stated goals of these programs is personal growth, the development of confidence and insight, the alleviation of symptoms, and the improvement of interpersonal relationships. The specific standards for *Wilderness and Adventure-Based Therapeutic Outdoor Services* include 20 areas that range from intake and assessment, treatment plans, family involvement, psychotherapy, and educational services. As an example, the standard concerning *Program Activities* is important because it helps ensure the well-being of participants, requiring that experiences be sequenced in terms of level of difficulty so that participants can succeed. The pace of the group can only be as fast as the slowest participant, and participants cannot be coerced into engaging in specific activities. The standard concerning *Service Philosophy, Modalities, and Interventions* provides safeguards by prohibiting corporal punishment, withholding food or water, physical exercise as punishment, and punishment by peers. Other standards govern personnel issues and staff training and development.

For example, the standards require that the mental health professional makes sure that any clinical services specified in a participant's service plan are carried out. Coordination and collaboration between the wilderness therapy program and outside providers is also mandated. The standards do not require that the mental health provider have a graduate degree in psychology, social work, or counseling. They do not require that the

mental health professional be licensed to practice or that the person have experience with wilderness therapy. The clinical director must have an advanced degree, but it can be in a field like experiential education, which does not necessarily include clinical training with troubled youth or mental health training. Course supervisors do not have to have any degrees or experience as supervisors. We believe that COA has set the bar surprisingly low for wilderness therapy programs that historically have taken on some of the most psychologically troubled youth, and we suggest that mental health providers in wilderness therapy programs should have the same level of credentials as do providers in programs that take a traditional approach.
Headquarters: New York
Website: www.coanet.org
Phone: 212-797-3000

The Joint Commission

The Joint Commission (until recently called the Joint Commission on the Accreditation of Healthcare Organizations or JCAHO) was founded in the 1950s to accredit hospitals. In 1972, it began accrediting mental health and substance abuse programs (JCAHO, 2002). Now, The Joint Commission accredits more than 1,800 programs in 17 program areas, ranging from addictions to corrections, from partial hospitalization to vocational rehabilitation, and from in-home counseling to outdoor programs. The Joint Commission defines behavioral health as "a broad array of mental health, chemical dependency, habilitation, and rehabilitation services provided in settings such as inpatient, day treatment, residential, and outpatient" (JCAHO, 2006, GL-3). (See Figure 5.1 at the end of this chapter for more about the commission's guiding principals.)

Wilderness therapy programs accredited by The Joint Commission must demonstrate compliance with the standards included in the the *Outdoor Programs* category of its accreditation manual. The standards for behavioral health programs are specified in this manual. Some important criteria for wilderness programs include the requirement that participant treatment plans are developed in conjunction with a participant's family. Safety is addressed by the standard that requires that all staff be trained to use restraints safely and as infrequently as possible. If and when restraints are used, their use must be approved by a state-licensed health provider who observes and evaluates the participant, and family is to be promptly notified. Certain procedures are prohibited, such as corporal punishment, the denial of basic needs, anything that elicits fear, or anything that hurts. The importance of these criteria is that they explicitly limit aversive aspects of programming.

The one aspect of The Joint Commission that, in our estimation, falls somewhat short concerns the qualifications of clinical staff. While we have advocated for independently licensed clinical staff to provide the treatment of participants while in the wilderness, The Joint Commission standards specify that the program leadership (e.g., administrators, policy-makers) determines the qualifications of staff. There are some limitations on the freedom of programs to set qualification levels in that staff must also be competent to perform their tasks and also have appropriate supervision (JCAHO, 2006). The Joint Commission, despite its apparent limitations in terms of staff qualifications, is commonly accepted as having the most stringent accreditation standards.

Headquarters: Illinois

Website: www.jointcommission.org

Phone: 630-792-5000

Credentialing in Other Countries

When researching programs outside of North America, warnings repeatedly pop up regarding the lack of regulation of wilderness programs in countries other than the United States and Canada. That is because numerous programs that have run into legal issues in countries that have regulatory measures end up moving their businesses to countries where regulation is lax or nonexistent. And while only the three organizations discussed in the previous section accredit wilderness therapy programs, per se, there are numerous associations based in other countries that accredit outdoor programs and individuals. One such organization is the Outdoor Council of Australia (OCA) which resulted from a merger in 2003 of the Australian Outdoor Education Council and the Outdoor Recreation Council of Australia. The stated purpose of this association is to support outdoor leaders, educators, and guides or the organizations that train them. The OCA strongly supports and promotes the idea of the evaluation and monitoring of programs (Outdoor Council of Australia, 2006; 2007). It publishes the *Australian Journal of Outdoor Education* and has a system in place for the registration of outdoor leaders (www.outdoorcouncil.asn.au/).

A second Australian system (the Adventure Activity Standards) for credentialing outdoor leaders has been established by the State of Victoria. There, credentialing through the Adventure Activity Standards is required for those who run programs on Crown land in Victoria as public land tour operators, or by those seeking an activity provider license (Outdoor Recreation Centre, 2007). The State of New South Wales also has a system of program certification through the Outdoor Recreation Industry Council (2007).

In 1996, Simon Crisp, a psychologist in Australia, completed an international investigation during which he observed therapeutic wilderness and wilderness therapy programs in the United Kingdom, the United States, and New Zealand (Crisp, 1996). His aim was to identify the best practices among wilderness therapy programs in order to create best practice guidelines for wilderness therapy programs in his home country. His study resulted in the development of the Wilderness Adventure Therapy Accreditation Scheme (Crisp, 2002; Crisp & Hinch, 2004), a national scheme that points the way toward professionalization of the wilderness therapy field in Australia.

In New Zealand, instructors must meet minimum standards in order to earn what is called "awards." These awards are distributed by the New Zealand Outdoor Instructors Association, a professional body for New Zealand outdoor instructors, and help to ensure that instructors possess required levels of competence in necessary areas (www.nzoia.org.nz/)

In Great Britain, Parliament passed the Activity Centres (Young Persons' Safety) Act in 1995 (Allison & Telford, 2005) after four adolescents died while sea kayaking as the result of inadequately trained staff and poorly planned programming. This act applies to programs for adolescents that charge a fee for participation or provide programs for educational institutions for youth. Programs that must be licensed include those that facilitate climbing, water sports, trekking, and caving (Adventure Activities Licensing Authority, 2004). This act requires that outdoor activity leaders be competent and show evidence of that competence (Woollven, Allison, & Higgins, 2006).

The credentialing in both Australia and Great Britain is largely limited to outdoor activities and not specifically to wilderness therapy. While they may increase the safety of adventure activities, they do not necessarily provide for more emotional safety for a mental health population. The one wilderness therapy accreditation program cited that does (Wilderness Adventure Therapy Scheme in Australia) is voluntary and has yet to be adopted on a large scale.

Credentialing of Individuals

Thus far, we have discussed state regulation, membership, and accreditation as they apply to programs. Another aspect of the credentialing issue concerns the qualifications of staff within these programs. (We briefly touched on this when we talked about the credentials that COA requires for various staff positions.) It is just as important to know about the qualifications of the wilderness therapy staff as it is to know about a program's adherence to certain standards. We explore this topic by considering clinical licensure and outdoor certifications. In order to support best practices, mental health therapists should possess the highest level of certification and/or licensure in their field. In the same way, staff involved in any of the outdoor aspects of the program should be fully trained and certified in various aspects of first aid. Those leading activities must be certified to lead those activities as well. We now examine some of these credentials in greater depth.

Clinical Licensure

Throughout the United States and in many other parts of the world, psychologists, social workers, and counselors must be licensed in order to practice in clinical settings. In fact, to call oneself a psychologist, social worker, or counselor, one generally must be licensed, because the use of these titles is governed by law. There are, however, exceptions to these rules. For example, a psychologist who teaches in a university setting and does not practice in a clinical setting can call him/herself a psychologist. A social worker who works for a child protection agency often does not have to have a degree in social work or be licensed in order to call him/herself a social worker. A counselor who works in a camp setting or does not work with mental health populations does not have to have a degree or license in order to practice, so camp counselors should not be confused with mental health counselors who have graduate degrees, supervised experience, and are licensed and/or certified.

Those exceptions not withstanding, mental health practitioners should be expected to have a license to practice in their state, province, or country. In the United States, each state has licensure boards that regulate the fields of psychology, social work, and counseling. Often there is a distinction between those who can practice independently and those who must practice under supervision (a "limited" license). In Ohio, for example, a person who obtains an undergraduate degree in social work may take an examination in order to become a licensed social worker (LSW). This level of licensure also can be attained after receiving a master's degree if the undergraduate degree was not in social work. The scope of practice with this LSW is limited, and the practice must be supervised. All LISWs must have master's degrees and have passed an advanced exam. Only LISWs are permitted to practice privately and receive health insurance reimbursement for their services. There is a similar situation for a licensed professional counselor (LPC) who has to be supervised by a licensed professional clinical counselor (LPCC). Different states use slightly different terms, such as LCSW (licensed clinical social worker), PCC (professional clinical counselor), and some states even have limited licenses for master's level psychologists.

While a person may be licensed in a specific jurisdiction (i.e., state, province), that does not give him/her the right to practice in another jurisdiction. Thus, even if we are licensed to practice our respective professions (social work and psychology) at the highest level in Ohio, we are not licensed to practice in any other state or country, unless we apply for and are granted a license to practice in that state or country. This law places significant constraints on wilderness therapy programs, as it precludes someone who is licensed in one state (say, Maine) to run a wilderness therapy trip in a neighboring state (say, Vermont), if s/he is not licensed in both states.

Another concern pertains to individuals with limited licenses that require them to practice under supervision. It might make sense for a person with a limited license (e.g., LSW or LPC) to work as a therapist in a community clinic where s/he can receive supervision on a regular basis, call his/her supervisor in the event of needed consultation or seek the backup services of a more well-trained individual on an emergency basis. On a wilderness therapy trip, the group may be many miles from civilization and out of reach of a supervisor (even satellite phones do not always work if there are clouds, or you're in a forest or in a canyon). Under those circumstances, the therapist must be able to function independently. For that reason, we strongly advocate that wilderness therapy programs employ only clinical staff who are licensed at the level that allows them to function independently and in the jurisdiction in which they are providing counseling. This idea is still contested as some argue that this level of credentialing is too difficult and costly to maintain in wilderness therapy programs.

While this position may need no explanation for those who are seeking a therapist in a community setting, it is the exception rather than the rule for wilderness counselors to be licensed mental health professionals and able to function on an independent level. This is increasingly more important for those programs that claim to be able to provide treatment for psychiatrically troubled individuals or that claim to provide mental health treatment.

Of the programs that employ fully credentialed mental health staff, only some send those staff into the field one or two times a week to hold group and individual therapy sessions. There are two problems with this approach. First, it assumes that the participants do not need therapy more often, even though the admission criteria for residential wilderness therapy programs includes the rationale that the participant is not able to function in the community with community resources. Second, it assumes the therapist is able to be effective when spending so little time in the wilderness with the participants.

Outdoor Certifications

Just as it is important to ensure that clinical staff are appropriately trained and credentialed, it is equally important that all wilderness staff are qualified outdoor leaders. Many wilderness therapy staff come to the wilderness therapy field with undergraduate degrees in outdoor recreation or similar majors that prepare them for outdoor leadership positions. Other times, students take courses that provide expertise, and sometimes certification, in a variety of outdoor skills as part of an undergraduate curriculum that isn't specifically related to outdoor recreation.

For those program activities that involve technical skills, the staff leading these activities should have the requisite documented training to carry out those activities. For example, if a participant in a wilderness therapy program were expected to engage in a canoeing experience in which they would be taught paddling skills, it is not unreasonable to expect that the program staff involved with this activity would have participated in an American Canoe Association (ACA) course at a higher level than the participants. In addition, the staff teaching the paddling skills should be certified canoe instructors (see the ACA website for details about courses and instructor certification www.acanet.org).

There are numerous ways to secure specific skill training that qualifies outdoor educators to take on field positions and lead certain activities. It is equally important that outdoor educators have training in wilderness medicine, because support for treatment of injuries in the field is often difficult to access. As such, CPR, wilderness first aid, and wilderness first responder courses are essential. Such training is offered by organizations such as the National Outdoor Leadership School (NOLS), Outward Bound (OB), and the Wilderness Education Association (WEA).

NOLS is the established leader in outdoor leadership education and offers a variety of ways for outdoor leaders to gain experience and certifications, ranging from 9-day backpacking leadership courses to semester-long trainings. NOLS also has a branch called the Wilderness Medicine Institute that offers more than 375 courses annually that focus on the recognition, treatment, and prevention of wilderness emergencies. While it is not the only program to offer these trainings, it is the largest, having trained more than 35,000 outdoor professionals in wilderness medicine. Staff leaders in a wilderness therapy program should have at least the Wilderness First Responder (WFR) credential. More information can be found at www.nols.edu.

Outward Bound offers Outward Bound Instructor Development courses that range from 22 to 50 days in the field. These are special-focus courses that teach outdoor leadership skills to participants who desire to lead Outward Bound and other wilderness trips. These courses instruct on how to lead a variety of outdoor activities, such as backpacking, climbing, and kayaking, and provide training in teaching and leadership. More information can be found at www.outwardbound.org.

The Wilderness Education Association offers training and certification in outdoor leadership through its network of 50 affiliates (www.weainfo.org). The cornerstone of WEA courses is the National Standard Program (NSP), a month-long course that teaches a standardized 18-point curriculum and leads successful candidates to become WEA-certified outdoor leaders.

Summary

Now that we have discussed the various credentialing, regulating, and accrediting bodies, we hope you feel ready to assess program credentials. To reiterate, there are state laws that regulate wilderness therapy programs, as well as professional membership associations, accrediting organizations, licensing laws for mental health professionals within each state, and certifications for outdoor professionals.

Even with a solid grasp of all the information this chapter covers, it can still be difficult for parents to choose a program for their child, for therapists to refer adolescents to good programs, and for reputable programs to distinguish themselves from the pack. We encourage you to be a good consumer and ask many questions. It is important to check with the authorities in the state in which the wilderness program is operating for information about staff, certifications, and accreditation status and to ascertain that programs do, in fact, have the licenses and accreditations they claim to. We believe that the future of wilderness therapy is rooted in issues of risk management, staff qualifications, and program licensure and certification. It is only through these avenues that wilderness therapy programs can begin to be recognized more readily by the mainstream mental health community. Remember, however, that credentials are not a guarantee of either program safety or effectiveness. However, we believe they can be a powerful tool in assessing the potential impact of a program.

Our next chapter reviews of some important research in the field of wilderness therapy. In language that is easy to understand, we present some of the basics of good research and then review key studies in the field.

Figure 5.1 Guiding principals of organizations discussed in Chapter 5.

Association for Experiential Education
"AEE is a nonprofit, professional membership association dedicated to experiential education and the students, educators, and practitioners who utilize its philosophy. We strive to: (1) Connect educators in practical ways so that they have access to the growing body of knowledge that fuels their growth and development; (2) Publish and provide access to relevant research, publications, and resources; (3) Raise the quality and performance of experiential programs through our accreditation program; (4) Increase recognition of experiential education worldwide." (www.aee.org)

The Council on Accreditation
"COA partners with human service organizations worldwide to improve service delivery outcomes by developing, applying, and promoting accreditation standards." (www.coanet.org)

The Joint Commission
"Our mission is to continuously improve the safety and quality of care provided to the public through the provision of health care accreditation and related services that support performance improvement in health care organizations." (www.jointcommission.org)

National Association of Therapeutic Schools and Programs
The members of NATSAP provide residential, therapeutic and/or education services to children, adolescents, and young adults entrusted to them by parents and guardians. The common mission of NATSAP members is to promote the healthy growth, learning, motivation, and personal well-being of program participants. The objective of NATSAP's therapeutic and educational programs is to provide excellent treatment for program participants; treatment that is rooted in concern for their well-being and growth; respect for them as human beings; and sensitivity to their individual needs and integrity." (www.natsap.org)

National Association of Therapeutic Wilderness Camps
"The primary purpose of NATWC is to support the establishment and continuation of therapeutic wilderness camping organizations; with the attendant responsibility to educate the public as to the existence of such organizations and their success in helping troubled young people change their lives for the better." (www.natwc.org)

Outdoor Behavioral Healthcare Industry Council
"OBHIC is an organization of behavioral health providers who are committed to the utilization of outdoor modalities to assist young people and their families to make positive change. OBHIC's mission is to unite its members and to promote the common good of our programs' standards and our industry at large. This mission has been accomplished by developing and policing the standards of excellence for membership and to have effective means of operating a service business by sharing and discussing thoughts and processes. By so doing, OBHIC will be the standard which families can trust for effectively assisting children and their families toward positive change." (Outdoor Behavioral Healthcare Industry Council, 2006)

References

Adventure Activities Licensing Authority. (2006). Inspecting standards of good practice. Retrieved August 18, 2006 from http://www.aala.org/

www.aee.org

Allison, P., & Telford, J. (2005). Turbulent times: Outdoor education in Great Britain 1993–2003. *Australian Journal of Outdoor Education, 9*(2), 21–30.

Berman, D., & Davis-Berman, J. (2001). Critical and emerging issues for therapeutic adventure. *Journal of Experiential Education, 24*, 68–69

Berman, D., & Davis-Berman, J. (2002). An integrated approach to crisis management in wilderness settings. *Journal of Adventure Education and Outdoor Learning , 2*(1), 9–17.

Berman, D., Davis-Berman, J., & Gillen, M. (1998). Behavioral and emotional crisis management in adventure education. *Journal of Experiential Education, 21*, 96–101.

www.coanet.org

Cooley, R. (1998). Wilderness therapy can help troubled adolescents. *International Journal of Wilderness, 4*(3), 18–22.

Cooley, R. (2000). OBHIC wilderness risk assessment incident report, year 2000. *Woodbury Reports*. Retrieved May 20, 2006 from www.strugglingteens.com.

Council on Accreditation. (2005). Group Living Services: 8th Edition Beta Standards 1.0 September 2005. Retrieved July 24, 2006 from http://www.coanet.org/files/Residential%20Standards.pdf .

Council on Accreditation. (2007). COA's service standards service definitions, 8th edition standards, beta version 1.0, February 2006. Retrieved July 28, 2006 from http://www.coanet.org/files/SvcDefinitions8thEd.pdf

Crisp, S. (1996). *International models of best practice in wilderness and adventure therapy: Implications for Australia*. Churchill Fellowship Report: Australia.

Crisp, S. (2002). *Australian Wilderness Adventure Therapy Accreditation Scheme*. Neo Publications: Melbourne, Australia.

Crisp, S., & Hinch, C. (2004). Treatment effectiveness of wilderness adventure therapy: Summary findings. Neo Publications: Melbourne, Australia. Retrieved August 18, 2006, from http://www.neopsychology.com

Davis-Berman, J., & Berman, D. (2002). Risk and anxiety in adventure programming. *Journal of Experiential Education, 25*, 305–310.

GAO. (2007). Residential treatment programs: Concerns regarding certain regarding abuse and death in certain programs for troubled youth. http://www.gao.gov/new.items/d08146t.pdf

Itin, C. (Ed.). (1998). *Exploring the boundaries of adventure therapy: International perspectives. Proceedings of the 1st international adventure therapy conference*. Perth, Australia.

www.jointcommission.org

Joint Commission on the Accreditation of Health Care Organizations. (2002). *How to chose a quality behavioral health provider*. Retrieved August 13, 2006 from http://www.jointcommission.org/NR/rdonlyres/9988195A-48EE-40A4-BED1-D83D38F87B9D/0/mktg_bhc_cy_brochure.pdf

Joint Commission on the Accreditation of Health Care Organizations. (2006). 2006–2007 *comprehensive accreditation manual for behavioral health care.* Oakbrook Terrace, IL: Author.

Krakauer, J. (October 1995). Loving them to death. *Outside Magazine.*

Leemon, D., Pace, S., Ajango, D., & Wood, H. (Eds.). (2005) *Manual of accreditation standards for adventure programs (4th Ed.).* Boulder, CO: Association for Experiential Education.

Leemon, D. (2006). Adventure program risk management report: Incident data from 1998–2005. Paper presented at the Wilderness Risk Management Conference, Killington, VT.

Luckner, J. L., & Nadler, R. S. (1997). *Processing the experience: Strategies to enhance and generalize learning.* Dubuque, IA: Kendall/Hunt.

Maslow, A. (1954). *Motivation and personality.* NewYork: Harper & Row.

Mitten, D. (1999). Leadership for community building. In J. Miles & S. Priest (EDs.). *Adventure programming* (pp. 253–261). State College, PA: Venture Publishing.

National Association of Therapeutic Wilderness Camps. (2006). Mission Statement. Retrieved June 9, 2006 from http://natwc.org

www.natsap.org

www.natwc.org

www.nols.edu

www.nzoia.org.nz

www.obhic.com

Oregon Department of Human Services. (2004). Oregon Administrative Rules 413-210-0800 thru 0883. In C*children, adults & families resource management manual II.*

Outdoor Behavioral Healthcare Industry Council. (2006). Mission Statement. Retrieved June 10, 2006, from http://www.obhic.com .

Outdoor Council of Australia (2007). National Outdoor Leader Registration Scheme: NOLRS version 2. Overview and Summary of Changes. Retrieved August 24, 2007, from http://www.outdoorcouncil.asn.au/

Outdoor Council of Australia. (2006). Statement of purpose. Retrieved August 7, 2006, from http://www.outdoorcouncil.asn.au/

Outdoor Recreation Industry Council (2007). ORIC Organisational Accreditation. Retrieved August 24, 2007 from http://www.oric.org.au/accreditationregistration/index.htm#

Outdoor Recreation Centre. (2007). Adventure activity standards. Retrieved August 18, 2006, from http://www.orc.org.au/aas/index.htm

www.outwardbound.org

Rogers, C. (1951). *Client-centered therapy.* Boston: Houghton Mifflin.

Russell, K. C., & Harper, R. (2006). Incident Monitoring in outdoor behavioral healthcare programs: A four-year summary of restraint, runaway, injury, and illness rates. *Journal of Therapeutic Schools and Programs, 1*(1), 70–90.

Schneider, H. G. (2007). GAO: Poor staffing cited in youths' deaths at 'Boot Camp.' Retrieved November 9, 2007 from http://www.washingtonpost.com/wp-dyn/content/article/2007/10/10/AR2007101000825.html?hpid=topnews

Szalavitz, M (2006). *Help at any cost: How the troubled-teen industry cons and hurts kids.* New York: Riverhead Books.

www.weainfo.org

Wood, H. Personal Communication. November 12, 2007.

Woodbury, L. (2007). Congressman Miller's drama. Retrieved November 9, 2007, from http://www.strugglingteens.com/artman/publish/CongMillerDramaES_071023.shtml

Woollven, R., Allison, P, & Higgins, P. (2007). Perception and reception: The introduction of licensing of adventure activities in Great Britain. *Journal of Experiential Education,* 30(1), 1–20.

CHAPTER 6

How Effective Is Wilderness Therapy?

When we look at websites or glossy advertisements published by wilderness therapy programs, most of them look great. They are filled with inviting pictures of participants who are working as part of a team, with happy faces, in beautiful locations. No program is going to show pictures of people shivering in cold or wet conditions, with participants acting out. After all, this advertising is no different than any other—its aim is to provide an enticing view of what the program wants us to see. This is not a criticism of wilderness therapy programs, just a fact about the nature of advertising.

So, how best to determine how well wilderness therapy programs work or if one program is better than another? There is no publication like *Consumer Reports* to consult, and there is no single standardized model for product testing as there is for prescription drugs.

Some of the best evaluative tools available to this market's consumers are the results of independent studies—some done by the programs themselves, as accreditation and credentialing efforts, others done by researchers in the field. In this chapter, we examine some of the recent research that has evaluated a variety of outdoor adventure programs, including some wilderness therapy programs. We begin by building a general rationale for the use of program evaluation, and then suggest how it might be used to evaluate wilderness therapy programs. We then provide overviews of two general approaches to program evaluation: qualitative and quantitative approaches. Next, we summarize the recent research on various forms of outdoor adventure programs, including wilderness therapy programs. And in the final section of this chapter we consider some of the challenges that confront the evaluation of wilderness therapy programs and conclude with a discussion of how research can be used to inform practice.

Many of the earlier studies on wilderness therapy were reviewed in our first book (Davis-Berman & Berman, 1994a). Because this book is written more for parents and professionals than academics, we discuss only those recent studies we believe have relevance to our audience. Any attempt to provide a comprehensive review of the literature would become quickly outdated and would require a depth of analysis that would not likely serve the purposes of our present audience. As with our chapter on recent programs, any omission of a study should not be interpreted as a judgment of its worth.

Why Do We Need Research?

Glossy ads may be enticing and personal testimonials can be moving, but objective data is the only way to accurately determine whether wilderness therapy, or a specific program, has the potential to help prospective clients. Programs are often eager to share personal or professional endorsements, such as letters of praise from clients, their families, or professionals, but is it wise to base a decision about one child's treatment on the success (or failure) of another child's experience? For example, the parents of a participant of a wilderness therapy program wrote to an administrator of the program saying, in part: "Words are just not powerful enough to thank you and each of the staff members ... for the wonderful job you all did in working with our son. If you've ever wondered, 'Do I make a difference?' we can unequivocally say that yes, you have made a difference, and for that we are grateful" (Hoyer and Hoyer, no date). Do the praises the parents sing about the program their son attended necessarily have implications for other youth being guided by other staff?

Similarly, should parents send their child to a particular wilderness therapy program because famed television psychologist Dr. Phil says: "I believe a lot in what you guys do" or that this program "is a very therapeutic program" (McGraw, 2005). There's no knowing whether Dr. Phil based his conclusion on his training in psychology, first-hand observation, a thorough review of the field, or simply impressions gleaned from some other experience. Whatever the source, testimonials and endorsements are too subjective to count on when making potentially life-changing decisions.

Some social scientists make a distinction between program evaluation and research. Put simply, research tends to be more theory oriented than does program evaluation. Research also tends to be more sophisticated, and more often uses complex statistical procedures. As such, research can be less directly applicable to program planners and practitioners than program evaluation can be, as it may focus on more basic than applied research questions (Lewis, Lewis, Packard, & Souflee, 2001). For our purposes, however, we will treat the results from both research and evaluation in a similar fashion, because we are looking for data that supports (or fails to support) wilderness therapy programs and, if there is general support, some substantiation of who this treatment works for, what changes can be expected, and the extent to which those changes can be sustained over time.

Types of Research

Quantitative research is most commonly used for program evaluation because of its reliance on empirical data and statistical analysis (Patton, 1987). The prototype for all quantitative research involves the double-blind experiment, in which there is an experimental group that gets a certain treatment and a control group that gets a placebo (i.e., an inert treatment that resembles the treatment but lacks the hypothetically critical elements necessary to create change) (Campbell & Stanley, 1963). Neither the subjects nor the researchers know which group a subject is in. The researchers measure objective data that is meant to reflect the positive changes that are the desired outcomes. That data is statistically analyzed so as to indicate the significance of any differences between the groups. Because this approach reflects the generally acceptable scientific method, one might deduce that it is the only model to apply to program evaluation, and that it is well suited for such an application.

There are some phenomena, however, that are not amenable to numerical measurement and require *qualitative types of research* methodologies (Patton, 1987). Such projects are characterized by the following: (1) They tend to take place in their natural environments rather than in laboratory settings. (2) The studies based on such projects do not begin with a framework or a theoretical perspective on a phenomenon; rather, they take an exploratory, inductive approach to the phenomena. (3) Qualitative research approaches involve active participation and require researchers actually go into the field and immerse themselves in the phenomena that is being evaluated. (4) Given that qualitative research approaches are phenomenological and not confined by a rigidly empirical focus, they are more flexible and holistic in their orientation (Patton, 1987, pp. 9–17). Qualitative research is of particular value to the field of wilderness therapy, as it allows researchers to actually observe the process of change, not just record the outcome.

Wilderness Therapy Research

A recent review of published empirical research from 1998 through 2003 on wilderness therapy was conducted by Keith Russell (2004), yielding six studies (four of which were conducted by Russell himself). Of the other two studies, one was on the effects of wilderness therapy on sex offenders (Lambie et al., 2000) and the other was on young adolescents (Brand, 2001). The latter study is not without some challenges to its methodology and conclusions (Crisp, 2003; Gray, 2003).

We followed Russell's procedure to update his review of recent research by using three search engines (PsychInfo, ERIC, and Academic Search Premiere) and searched the recent issues of the *Journal of Experiential Education, Journal of Adventure Education*, and the *Australian Journal of Outdoor Education*. Our search was limited to empirical studies of wilderness therapy or adventure therapy that focused on the process or outcome of treatment. While Russell (2004) also looked at unpublished dissertations, we omitted dissertations, limiting our search to published, peer-reviewed journals (a commonly accepted standard for scholarly works). We also included one study that was reported in an edited conference proceeding (Mossman & Goldthorpe, 2004).

One study compared outdoor adventure programs to group home programs for adolescents in the juvenile justice system (Jones, Lowe, & Risler, 2004) and found no difference in recidivism (reoffense) rates between wilderness therapy and group homes. Lan, Sveen, and Davidson (2004) also conducted a study that looked at recidivism rates following participation in an outdoor adventure program. Using a pre-, post-, and two-year follow-up design for adolescents from a number of community agencies, moderate effects were found on measures of increased self-actualization and decreased hopelessness. Three-fourths of the youth who had prior court offenses did not reoffend at follow-up; but a third of those adolescents with no court involvement had received convictions at follow-up. There was no control group with which to compare these results.

In a study using adolescents from both wilderness therapy and day treatment school settings, Bickman et al. (2004) looked at the therapeutic alliance between adolescents and their counselors, based on the premise that the relationship between counselors and clients is predictive of clinical outcomes. They found little agreement between counselors' ratings and adolescents' ratings of the therapeutic relationship.

High-school dropouts who were enrolled in a special program in Israel were studied by Romi and Kohan (2004). They compared wilderness therapy, a residential program, and the standard treatment for enrollees in this program. Their measures included self-concept and locus of control. In general, both treatment groups showed gains in self-concept when compared to the standard treatment, but no differences in locus of control.

An intriguing study by Clark, Marmol, Cooley, and Gathercoal (2004) looked at the diagnostic characteristics of 109 adolescents successively admitted to a wilderness therapy program. Clark et al. took measures on two psychological instruments, a personality inventory and a behavior rating scale, in order to study which diagnostic categories of adolescents might best be helped by wilderness therapy and the extent to which defensive personality styles might be altered by wilderness therapy. They found positive change for a range of diagnoses and personality styles. Improvements were particularly large for participants who were introverted, inhibited and avoidant, depressive, submissive, egocentric, forceful, conforming, oppositional, and self-demeaning. In the absence of a control group, however, it is not possible to make wide generalizations about efficacy.

Mossman and Goldthorpe (2004) reported on a study connected with a New Zealand mental health program supported by government regional health funding. In this program, adolescents referred for mental health and substance abuse problems participated in weekly therapy appointments as well as a 9-day wilderness therapy trek. Using a repeated-measures design with no control group, objective tests were administered to participants before, after, and at follow-up involvement in this program. The results indicated significant improvement in overall adjustment, as well as acting out (externalizing) and mood (internalizing), such that participants went from scores in the clinical range to the normal range. That is, the average participant's scores on total problems on the Child Behavior Checklist went from approximately the 95th percentile before the program to the 60th percentile at follow-up. The results also suggested that the use of alcohol and drugs significantly declined. One measure of this is the fact that while more than one half of the participants met the *DSM-IV* criteria for a substance abuse disorder before the program, less than 16% met the same criteria after the program.

Young children between the ages of 9 and 11 were shown to have an increase in self-concept scores, as compared to a control group, following participation in a Life Adventure Camp program. Although potentially interesting, it is not clear what this camp involved and whether therapy of any kind took place (Larson, 2007).

Three other important research studies published by Keith Russell (Russell, 2005; Russell & Sibthorp, 2004; Caulkins, White, & Russell, 2006) are worth discussing. One of these studies (Russell, 2005), a follow-up study of wilderness therapy participants, will be presented in the next section of this chapter. Another (Russell & Sibthorp, 2004) reported on the use of a sophisticated statistical technique to look at program outcomes. Applying this technique, the authors concluded that wilderness therapy programs that are longer may be more effective and that females may benefit more than males, although the factors that account for this difference were not elucidated. These findings, using innovative methods for data analysis, replicate those found earlier by Russell (2003) in which more traditional research methods were used. The third study (Caulkins, White, & Russell, 2006) used qualitative methodology to look at the impact backpacking had on young women in a wilderness therapy program. This will be discussed in the qualitative research section of this chapter.

Other recent studies have looked at the impact of wilderness therapy programs on special populations. For example, a wilderness therapy program in Norway connected with an inpatient psychiatric program was compared to a traditional inpatient program. All of the patients treated had been diagnosed with avoidant personality disorder. Although the results suggested that there were no significant differences between the groups after treatment, participation in the wilderness therapy program did shorten the length of treatment (Eikenaes, Gude, & Hoffart, 2006). This research is important, because there are not many generally accepted treatments for this type of personality disorder.

Voruganti et al. (2006) reported on a program that allowed participants with schizophrenia to participate in wilderness activities during both a summer and winter session. Compared to the control group, the treatment group showed a significant increase in self-esteem and global functioning at the end of the program. These changes were still evident 12 months after program completion. Interestingly, the treatment group also lost an average of 12 pounds, while the control group gained an average of 9 pounds. This study is notable in that outdoor treatment approaches are rarely used with people with schizophrenia. In fact, most programs exclude participants with this disorder. Although these results are interesting, this study is not specifically about wilderness therapy, and the authors do not discuss whether any type of therapy actually took place.

Another study looked at the impact of an outdoor adventure program on participants with cognitive disabilities. This study is important in that this is another group that is not often served by outdoor adventure programs. After participating in a short outdoor adventure program, participants reported high satisfaction with the trip, increased outdoor skills and, most importantly, an increase in social/socialization skills (McAvoy, Smith, & Rynders, 2006).

The therapeutic outfitting model of trekking was applied in Canada to develop a model to incorporate wilderness experiences into the mental health system serving adolescents. This program involved intervention over at least a 6-month period, and included team building, experiential activities, and outdoor skills training. This training was followed by a wilderness trip, such as sea kayaking or hiking. This approach is interesting in that most of the clients have already been in therapy, multiple interventions take place over a 6-month period, it is used as an adjunctive treatment, and it can be used as a preventative approach to mental health (Harper & Scott, 2006). This model holds great promise in Canada, and the results of the evaluation of this program are forthcoming.

A study by Jelelian and colleagues (2006) is an example of the use of excellent research methodology. Although the program they studied is not a wilderness therapy program but rather an outdoor adventure offering, we discuss it in more depth because of the high caliber of its methodology. It included 76 adolescents who were 20% to 80% overweight and who were randomly assigned to either a 16-week wilderness trip or an exercise group (both groups also received cognitive behavioral therapy). Measures were taken at the start of the program, at the end of the 16-week program, and 10 months after the start of the program. This study included some of the standard psychosocial measures (e.g., self-concept) as well as weight loss, a measure that was easily quantifiable. The results indicated that both groups lost significant amounts of weight and performed equally well at the end of treatment. At the end of the 16-week program, the wilderness group lost an average of 5.3 kilograms (11.7 pounds), and the exercise group lost an average of 3.3 kilograms (7.3 pounds). The study also revealed that among older adolescents, the wilderness trip group lost four times as much weight as the exercise group.

The methodology employed by this study (Jelelian et al., 2006) makes it a model for future outdoor adventure program research. Its defining elements are: (1) clear criteria (subjects were at least 20% overweight); (2) the random assignment of participants to treatment groups; (3) and objective, standardized measures were taken before, after, and at follow-up for all subjects.

OBHRC Studies

As we have mentioned in other chapters, the Outdoor Behavioral Healthcare Research Cooperative (OBHRC) has done a number of research studies on treatment effectiveness. One of its first studies (Russell, 2003) assessed the effectiveness of wilderness therapy by taking a series of objective measures on 523 participants and 372 parents before and after their enrollment in eight OBHIC programs. The results indicated a reduction in emotional and behavioral symptoms following completion of the program. This change was true for both participants and their parents on the Youth Outcome Questionnaire scales measuring behavior disorders, substance disorders, and mood disorders. These gains were maintained at follow-up 1 year later.

The second study (Russell, 2005) was a 2-year follow-up of the 2003 study. In data collected in phone interviews, the vast majority of those contacted believed that treatment was effective (more than 80% of parents and 90% of participants). While some participants clearly had improved, the majority had had run-ins with the law (60%) and used alcohol and/or drugs (74%) after participating in OBHIC programs. On a more positive note, 84% of the participants remained in therapy after enrollment in the Outdoor Behavioral Healthcare Council program.

A major study was done on an OBHIC program in the Northwest, resulting in two publications (Harper & Cooley, 2007; Harper, Russell, Cooley, & Cupples, 2007). Parents of wilderness therapy participants were surveyed at pretest and at 2 and 12 months posttest. This study generated a great deal of data. It described some of the major problem areas of participants, and looked at gender differences in problem areas both before and after the program. In summary, both males and females were seen to improve in their functioning after participation in a wilderness therapy trip, based on the assessments of their parents. However, when looking at areas of functioning at 12-month follow-up, changes in the family context were not as stable as changes in some other areas. Although data other than family impact was collected, the authors' conclusion that more attention needs to be paid to the family system as programs are designed, run, and evaluated is particularly interesting.

In Russell's 2006 study, a Canadian OBHIC program geared toward adjudicated youth was evaluated. While this program includes elements of a traditional residential program, approximately 40% of the time is spent on expedition. A standardized instrument was used to look at areas like intrapersonal distress, interpersonal relationships, social problems and behavioral dysfunction. From pre- to posttest, the scores decreased, indicating less distress. These changes were especially dramatic in the areas of interpersonal relations and social problems. Finally, the youth rated the program very highly. The school program, challenge activities, and staff were rated as the best parts of the program (Russell, 2006).

Meta-Analysis

A promising recent technique for analyzing the effects of treatments is meta-analysis. Simply stated, this statistical technique provides a way of comparing the results of different studies to obtain the "size of the effect" of a given treatment. Thus, a meta-analysis statistically provides a way of determining the strength of a treatment (the independent variable) on measurable outcomes (dependent variables) by combining the results (effect sizes) of several studies that address a set of related research hypotheses. This technique is used when studies have a small number of subjects, differing comparison groups (e.g., when some studies have no control group and others do), or when different studies use different outcome measures. A treatment that had no effect would have an effect size (ES) of 0. Effect sizes in the range of 0.2 are considered small or educationally significant, and those in the range of 0.5 are considered moderate or of practical significance, and 0.8 is considered large. It is even possible to obtain an effect size in the negative range if a treatment results in a reduced numerical outcome (Cohen, 1988).

Neill (2002) reviewed the meta-analyses of five studies that were generally aimed at looking at the effects of outdoor education programs. The largest of these studies (Hattie, Marsh, Neill, & Richards, 1997) considered 97 studies with a total of more than 12,000 adolescent and adult participants before and after a range of outdoor education programs. The ES found by Hattie et al. was in the small-to-moderate range (0.34). Another study reviewed by Neill (2002) was notable because it found a very low ES of 0.2 for the outcome of camping programs (Marsh, 1999). Neill found the highest ES, 0.55, for the effects of challenge courses on teamwork and self-concept (Bunting & Donley, 2002). Taken as a whole, these meta-analyses suggest a small-to-moderate improvement in such measures as leadership, interpersonal skills, self-concept, and academic outcomes (Neill, 2002). (Note that these studies did not focus on wilderness therapy programs.)

When we inquire about the effect size for wilderness therapy programs, the results are less clear. The ESs for wilderness therapy programs have little meaning unless they are compared to the ESs for more traditional treatment. The ES for adolescent psychotherapy patients has been reported to be 0.71 (Casey & Berman, 1985). This is the best number to compare to the effect sizes reported in the meta-analyses of outdoor education experiences. Remember that outdoor education can encompass a wide variety of activities for many types of adolescents, including well-adjusted, average, gifted, clinical, and delinquent populations. Looking at these measures, Neill (2003) found ESs ranging from 0.24 on measures of well-being to 1.05 on an undefined collection of "clinical measures" in the meta-analysis by Cason and Gillis (1992). Neill cautions the reader by saying meta-analyses "may unwittingly contribute to overestimating adventure therapy program effectiveness" (p. 320) because published data may not be representative of what is happening in most programs.

Qualitative Studies

Quantitative studies, like those cited in the previous section, can tell us which factors are statistically significant in terms of their relationship to each other, but often fail to elucidate the nature of the relationship. For example, Russell and Sibthorp (2004) found a statistical relationship between gender and outcome that led them to conclude that female participants showed greater improvements than male participants. Even if this finding is one that stands the test of being robust (its ability to be replicated by other studies), the study doesn't tell us what it is about wilderness therapy that makes women more amenable to change. Qualitative studies are best suited to answer such questions.

There are many varieties of approaches to qualitative research, with equally varied methods of qualitative data analysis (Neuman, 1997). Qualitative research is less abstract in that the data is based on the raw data of language and behavior, not the inferred statistical analyses used in quantitative approaches.

There are few qualitative studies that provide insight into wilderness or adventure therapy. One such study was recently conducted by Sugarman (2005), who interviewed four cancer survivors after they participated in a challenge course. These interviews were semistructured, recorded, transcribed, and analyzed for themes. The results revealed three primary themes: improved sense of self, feelings of support, and increased control. In that this study was qualitative, we may gain insight into what was important to participants, but the magnitude of the effect cannot be determined in terms of percentage of change or other measures that could be obtained from quantitative research. Studies like this help identify the process that leads to growth. (Note that this was not a wilderness therapy experience but a challenge course experience.)

One of the most ambitious qualitative studies to date was conducted by Russell (2005). In this qualitative study, short phone interviews were conducted with 88 parents and 47 youth who participated in wilderness therapy programs 2 years earlier (Russell, 2003). They were asked about the current well-being of the youth and their involvement in therapy in the 2 years following participation in wilderness therapy programs. Their responses were transcribed into text for analysis. From this data, themes were gleaned and data were analyzed using a computer program for qualitative data. Six themes were identified as to why this treatment was effective: Being Away, Group Peers, Nature Primitive, Program, Sense of Self, and Staff Support (Russell, 2005, p. 218). Actual quotes from respondents further elucidated the transformative process, providing richness and detail. Respondents indicated that being away from their usual environment was restorative. Spending time with a group of their peers was also important to the success of the program. Being out in the natural environment was healing and helped shape a sense of self. Finally, the support of staff and relationships with the staff on the trip were pivotal. Qualitative studies such as Russell's are important because they bring to life the numbers generated in quantitative studies and provide information about the process of change.

In the previously summarized study by Mossman and Goldthorpe (2004), subjects were asked to describe factors they believed most led to positive change. The three factors mentioned were themes related to themselves (e.g., motivation, expectations), to their counselors (e.g., trust, respect), and the program (e.g., the wilderness therapy trek). The qualitative data analysis in this study was less rigorous than in some other studies, but the findings are consistent with those found elsewhere.

To provide an idea about the range of possibilities for qualitative research, consider a recent study by Loeffler (2005). Subjects in this study were college students who participated in outdoor programs. They brought their cameras on trips and, to participate in this research, shared their pictures and agreed to be interviewed. Using their pictures, subjects were asked to talk about the meaning of their experiences. Three themes emerged, suggesting that students gained a sense of being spiritually connected to nature, connected with peers, and engaged in self-discovery and reflection. This novel approach presents yet another way in which researchers attempt to determine what factors lead to growth in the wilderness.

Another qualitative study worth mentioning was conducted on an OBHIC program in the southwestern United States. This study looked at the emotional, cognitive, and physical impacts of backpacking on six adolescent females. Data was collected through direct observation, interviews, and participant documentation. General and substantive impacts were identified. The general impacts of the backpacking experience were found to be: (1) reflection, (2) perceived competence, and (3) accomplishment. More substantive impacts were: (1) self-efficacy, (2) awareness of surroundings, self, and others, and (3) timelessness (Caulkins, White, & Russell, 2006).

Challenges to Wilderness Therapy Research

There are aspects of wilderness therapy that make conducting research on programs especially difficult. Some of these challenges are discussed in the following paragraphs.

Homogeneity of Subjects

When conducting research, it is important to select a group of participants (subjects) for whom the treatment is hypothesized to work. Lack of clarity about the characteristics of the subject pool creates a situation where even the most seemingly conclusive outcomes don't decisively reveal who benefits from the treatment. Programs that want to demonstrate their effectiveness should group participants according to the similar challenges or issues they bring to the program. Research done on programs that claim to be effective for many types of participants tell us very little, if anything, about who is really being helped.

Take, for example, one program that says it can help the following population:

- Males and females
- 13–17 years old
- Poor family and peer relationships
- Risky, irresponsible behaviors (drug/alcohol use, sex, running away)
- Not performing to potential
- Low self-esteem, depressed
- Isolating, withdrawn, underdeveloped social skills
- Poor understanding of consequences, entitled
- Poor academic performance, truancy
- Oppositional defiance, lack of respect for authority
- ADD/ADHD
- Minimal compassion, empathy for others
- Behaviors in contradiction to family values

Even if this program could show positive outcomes for adolescents facing any of these issues, it would be impossible to gauge to whom the results apply. The description is simply too broad. At some point or another, almost every adolescent would manifest at least one of the behaviors cited on the list. On the other hand, if the program intends its list to qualify only those adolescents who exhibit *all* of these behaviors, very few candidates would exist (but at least in that case we'd have a good idea of who the program aims to help).

The point is that in order for research results to be applicable— that is, in order to gauge how well a particular population is served by a program—programs being studied must group participants according to the challenges they face. Few, if any, programs can meet this research criteria. Most strive to help those who have a range of problems that have been unsuccessfully treated in traditional outpatient settings.

Sample Size

The average wilderness therapy trip involves six to eight participants. It takes lots of participants to constitute a group large enough to perform statistical analyses. How many participants is enough? That depends on the effectiveness of the treatment. Powerful treatments are evident with fewer subjects. However, more is usually better. To generate statistically valid results, data needs to be taken on a number of wilderness therapy trips and then combined to create a larger database.

One promising approach was taken by the aforementioned group of researchers (Clark, Marmol, Cooley, & Gathercoal, 2004) who looked at the diagnostic characteristics of 109 adolescents who were successively admitted to a wilderness therapy program. These adolescents were given a variety of objective psychological tests before and after going on a trip. Of particular interest is the fact that these researchers attempted to clinically describe trip participants in terms of measurable diagnostic criteria. They also used a fairly large sample. While certain aspects of this study have helped pinpoint which types of problems wilderness therapy is able to address, the study has its shortcomings, as addressed in the next section about control groups.

Control Groups

The presence of an appropriate control group is a cornerstone of quantitative research. Consider the study just cited (Clark et al., 2004), in which there was no control group, a problem acknowledged by the authors. Having no control group makes it virtually impossible to determine the meaning of the significant pre-to-posttest changes found in this study. There was a significant decline in maladaptive behavior (measured by a standardized inventory completed by parents) scores from the beginning to the end of the study; however, it is not possible to know if this is due merely to the passage of time, the program treatment, or simply because the subjects took the test twice. It is also not possible to know how subjects would score on these measures if they were in traditional therapy, or on medication only, or in any one of a number of other therapeutic modalities. Thus the importance of a control group. Of course, we realize that control groups are particularly difficult to construct and use in wilderness programs where enrollment is continual and often fluid. It is much easier to construct these groups within traditional treatment programs where enrollment is stable and predictable.

A related issue concerns the nature of the control group. In the traditional double-blind study, one group gets the treatment and the other group gets a placebo. Often, however, the proper comparison is the traditional treatment. In other words, it might be more important to compare wilderness therapy to other therapies (e.g., outpatient counseling) rather than to no counseling.

Longitudinal Data

Not only are we interested in whether or not participants in wilderness therapy programs change while they are in the program but, perhaps even more importantly, whether the changes will last over time. Also, will they be maintained no matter the situation in which a subject finds her/himself once s/he returns home? These questions have to do with the stability of change. In order to justify separating the adolescents from family and community, not to mention the expense of the program, changes should be made when enrolled in the program and be maintained when the participant goes home.

Determining the wilderness therapy's lasting effect is difficult for a number of reasons. First, participants often enroll in aftercare programs in their home communities following completion of a wilderness therapy program. When these participants are studied 6 or even 12 months after finishing a wilderness program, it is difficult to determine if their level of current functioning is a result of the wilderness program, the aftercare experience, or a whole host of other variables, including the simple passage of time. Also, staying in contact with program participants is often not easy, making follow-up studies difficult to conduct. People move, change names, and past participants often can't be located after a few years.

Limited Data Gathering

The wilderness provides a wonderful backdrop for therapeutic programs, but it can make data gathering a challenge. Some instruments are computer administered, rendering field administration impossible. Other instruments involve recorded observations by trained researchers who often don't have access to participants while they are in the field. Some instruments involve the use of booklets or other materials that cannot be easily carried into the field. These limitations dictate the types of instruments that are used or the time frames in which measures are recorded. Thus, it is often easier to administer a pencil-and-paper depression test before, during, and after a trip, which doesn't always yield the most accurate results and makes doing qualitative research on wilderness therapy programs difficult.

The Nature of the Treatment

Wilderness therapy programs are complex in that they involve a variety of components that range from exposure to the natural environment and group therapy, to modeling, journaling, the use of metaphors, and a host of other variables. Even if research shows that people experience positive transformation as the result of a program, it is difficult to assess which elements of the program are responsible for such changes. Moreover, research studies often don't adequately detail what constituted the treatment. Without this kind of detail, it is not possible for others to replicate the conditions under which the research study found changes.

Another limitation on the nature of the treatment concerns the fact that most studies focus on the outcome of the trip and not the process of change that participants undergo. Defining the process of change is most readily done via qualitative studies which, unfortunately, are often more time consuming, invasive, and expensive.

In summary, there are serious challenges to identifying which aspects of wilderness therapy work, for whom they work, and how they work. Challenges include the lack of homogeneity of subjects, small sample sizes, lack of control groups, lack of longitudinal research studies, limited ability to gather data in the field (noninvasively), and the multidimensional nature of treatments in wilderness therapy programs. These research limitations are applicable not just to wilderness therapy, but have also been discussed with regard to the larger field of experiential education (Ewert, 2005).

How Research Informs Practice

A promising approach to research is to follow the path of an evidence-based practice model promoted by the medical profession (Institute of Medicine, 2001) and the field of psychology (APA Presidential Task Force on Evidence-Based Practice, 2006). Evidence-based practice is "the conscientious, explicit, and judicious use of current best evidence in making decisions about the care of individual[s]" by integrating "clinical expertise with the best available external clinical evidence from systematic research" (Sackett, Rosenberg, Gray, Haynes, & Richardson, 1996, p. 71). By embracing such an approach, the field of wilderness therapy would improve the care of participants and, at the same time, enhance its image as an effective modality of treatment (Crisp, 2004; Newes, 2001). The place to start is with the best research evidence. Through this research, treatment manuals can be developed that describe the therapeutic and clinical elements of treatment. This information can then be used to promote program evaluation and development.

Another component of evidence-based practice relates to clinical expertise. Part of that expertise is built on the evaluation and use of research, as mentioned above. Other aspects of this expertise include identifying those individual programs that have good outcomes, as well as which treatments work, and for whom they work. Being particular and specific about the types of problems and individuals best served by wilderness therapy contributes to evidence-based practice. Finally, there needs to be an examination of research evidence as it relates to clinical expertise, as neither is effective in the absence of the other.

Individuals trying to make decisions about wilderness therapy programs are often bombarded by research data. We have tried to present, in clear language, examples of the kind of information that research studies can yield. In doing research for this book, we found that while there have been advances in the sophistication of research on wilderness therapy since the publication of our first book, methodology continues to compromise findings. That said, research results are favorable toward the field. Specifically, wilderness therapy appears to be helpful in elevating self-concept, decreasing psychiatric symptoms, improving social skills, lowering recidivism, and reducing substance abuse. There is some consistency in the findings that report at least some of these results are lasting ones. The power (effect size) of these findings ranges from low to moderate and may even approach that of traditional therapy for adolescents. The following chart offers a summary of the findings supported by research, and those not supported by research.

Findings Supported by Research	Claims Unsupported by Research
Improved self-concept	Treatment more effective than traditional modalities
Improved social skills	A prevention for suicide
Fewer psychiatric symptoms	Alleviation of depression or other major psychiatric problems
Decreased alcohol and substance abuse	Respect for authority
Lowered recidivism	Academic success
Improved academics	

It is our belief that before absolute confidence can be placed in the research that shows positive transformation as a result of wilderness therapy, more emphasis needs to be placed on methodological issues. In order for research to be considered legitimate, it must be able to be replicated. For this to occur, it is necessary that there be a more homogeneous population of participants with well-specified diagnostic criteria. An example of this would be to conduct a study with subjects who meet the DSM-IV criteria for alcohol abuse. There would also have to be a random assignment of subjects in treatment and control groups. Next, wilderness therapy would have to be specified in terms of the activities, procedures, and the structure of the program, so that it is clear what kinds of programming yield which results. More emphasis also needs to be placed on having objective measures of change that have statistical properties that are valid and reliable. (See Figure 6.1 for these recommendations.)

Given the results summarized in this chapter, and the caveats discussed, it is reasonable to be optimistic but cautious when we consider the effectiveness of wilderness therapy programs. When conducting a cost-benefit analysis of what is likely to help adolescents, there is widespread support for improvements in self-concept, with low risks (or costs) for programs aimed at adolescents who could use a boost in self-esteem. On the other hand, there is less support for using wilderness therapy as an alternative to traditional mental health programs that deal with severe behavioral problems. And, of course, there's the issue of cost to consider (some wilderness therapy programs charge as much as $15,000 per month), as well as the fact that wilderness therapy programs separate the adolescent from family and community support. For those programs (including wilderness therapy programs) with less clear benefits when compared to costs (or risks), the decision of whether or not to enroll has to be made on other criteria than pure research.

Studies need to be replicated.

Homogenous population groups help identify which types of people the treatment helps.

Random assignment to treatment and control groups is desirable.

Program elements, activities, and structure should be well defined.

Objective measures should be valid and reliable.

Figure 6.1 *Research recommendations.*

In Chapter 7, we move from discussions of theory and research to a review of the types of programs available, as well as descriptions of a number of specific programs, to provide readers with an overview of the variety of options that are available.

References

APA Presidential Task Force on Evidence-Based Practice. (2006). Evidence-based practice in psychology. *American Psychologist, 61,* 271–285.

Bickman, L., De Andrade, A. R. V., Lambert, E. W., Doucette, A., Sapyta, J., Boyd, A. S., Rumberger, D. T., Moore-Kurnot, J., McDonough, L. C., & Rauktis, M. B. (2004). Youth therapeutic alliance in intensive treatment settings. *Journal of Behavioral Health Services & Research, 31,*134–148.

Brand, D. (2001). A longitudinal study of the effects of a wilderness-enhanced program on behavior-disordered adolescents. *Australian Journal of Outdoor Education, 6,* 40–56.

Bunting, C. J., & Donley, J. P. (2002, January). *Ten years of challenge course research: A review of affective outcome studies.* Poster presented at the 6th Biennial Coalition for Education in the Outdoors Research Symposium, Bradford Woods, IN.

Campbell, D., & Stanley, J. (1963). *Experimental and quasi-experimental designs for research.* Boston, MA: Houghton Mifflin.

Casey, R. J., & Berman, J. S. (1985). The outcome of psychotherapy with children. *Psychological Bulletin, 98,* 388–400.

Cason, D., & Gillis, H. L. (1992). A meta-analysis of outdoor adventure programming with adolescents. *Journal of Experiential Education, 17,* 40–47.

Caulkins, M., White, D., & Russell, K. (2006). The role of exercise in wilderness therapy for troubled adolescent women. *Journal of Experiential Education, 29,* 18–37.

Clark, J. P., Marmol, L. M., Cooley, R., & Gathercoal, K. (2004). The effects of wilderness therapy on the clinical concerns (on Axes I, II, and IV) of troubled adolescents. *Journal of Experiential Education, 27,* 213–232.

Cohen, J. (1988). *Statistical power analysis for the behavioral sciences* (2nd edition). Hillsdale, NJ: Erlbaum.

Crisp, S. (2003). Publishing spurious research findings won't build a profession: Response to Brand's (2001) evaluation of the Wilderness Enhanced Program. *Australian Journal of Outdoor Education, 7,* 52–57

Crisp, S. (2004). Envisioning the birth of a profession: A blue-print of evidence based, ethical, best practice. In. S. Bandoroff & S. Newes (Eds.). *Coming of age: The evolving field of adventure therapy* (pp. 209–223). Boulder, CO: Association for Experiential Education.

Davis-Berman, J., & Berman, D. (1994a). *Wilderness therapy: Foundations, theory and research.* Dubuque, IA: Kendall/Hunt.

Davis-Berman, J., & Berman, D. (1994b). Research update: Two year follow-up report for the Wilderness Therapy Program. *Journal of Experiential Education, 17,* 48–50.

Eikenaes, I., Gude, T., & Hoffart, A. (2006). Integrated wilderness therapy for avoidant personality disorder. *Nordic Journal of Psychiatry, 60,* 275–281.

Ewert, A. (2005) Reflections on experiential education and the Journal: Possible pathways to the future. *Journal of Experiential Education, 28,* viii–xi.

Gray, T. (2003). Reply to Crisp: Blinkered perceptions lead to "spurious" viewpoints. *Australian Journal of Outdoor Education, 7,* 58.

Harper, N., & Cooley, R. (2007). Parental reports of adolescent and family well-being following a wilderness therapy intervention: an exploratory look at systemic change. *Journal of Experiential Education, 29*(3), 393–396.

Harper, N., Russell, K., Cooley, R., & Cupples, J. (2007). Catherine Freer Wilderness therapy Expeditions: An exploratory case study of adolescent wilderness therapy, family functioning, and the maintenance of change. *Child Youth Care Forum, 36,* 111–129.

Harper, N., & Scott, D. (2006). Therapeutic outfitting: Enhancing conventional adolescent mental health interventions through collaborations with a wilderness experience programme. *Therapeutic Communities: International Journal for Therapeutic and Supportive Organizations, 27*(4), 549–571.

Hatttie, J. M., Marsh, H. W., Neill, J. T., & Richards, G. E. (1997). Adventure education and Outward Bound: Out-of-class experiences that have a lasting effect. *Review of Educational Research, 67,* 43–87.

Hoyer, M., & Hoyer, T. (no date) Letter to the editor. Retrieved January 6, 2006 from http://www.strugglingteens.com/news/lettertoeditor/tammy_markVQ051130.htm

Institute of Medicine. (2001). *Crossing the quality chasm: A new health system for the 21st century.* Washington, DC: National Academies Press.

Jelalian, E., Mehlenbeck, R., Lloyd-Richardson, E. E., Birmaher, V., & Wing, R. R. (2006). 'Adventure therapy' combined with cognitive-behavioral treatment for overweight adolescents. *International Journal of Obesity, 30,* 31–39.

Jones, C. D., Lowe, L.A., Risler, E. A. (2004). The effectiveness of wilderness adventure therapy programs for young people involved in the juvenile justice system. *Residential Treatment for Children & Youth, 22,* 53–62.

KidsQuest Wagon Train (no date). Student profile. Retrieved January 6, 2006 from http://www.vq.com/kidsquest/Articles/StudentProfile.html

Lambie, I., Hickling, L., Seymour, F., Simmonds, L., Robson, M., & Houlahan, C. (2000). Using wilderness therapy in treating adolescent sexual offenders. *Journal of Sexual Aggression, 5*, 99–117.

Lan, P., Sveen, R., & Davidson, J. (2004). A Project Hahn empirical replication study. *Australian Journal of Outdoor Education, 8*, 37–43.

Larson, B. (2007). Adventure camp programs, self-concept, and their effects on behavioral problem adolescents. *Journal of Experiential Education, 29(3)*, 313–330.

Lewis, J. A., Lewis, M. D., Packard, T., & Souflee, F. (2001). *Management of human service programs* (3rd Ed.). Belmont, CA: Brooks/Cole.

Loeffler, T. A. (2005). Looking deeply in: Using photo-elicitation to explore meanings of outdoor education experiences. *Journal of Experiential Education, 27*, 343–346.

Marsh, P. E. (1999). *What does camp do for kids? A meta-analysis of the influence of organized camping experience on the self-constructs of youth.* Unpublished master's thesis, Department of Recreation and Park Administration, Indiana University.

McAvoy, L., Smith, J., & Rynders, R. (2006). Outdoor adventure programming for individuals with cognitive disabilities who present serious accommodation challenges. *Therapeutic Recreation Journal, 40(3)*, 182–199.

McGraw, P. (2005). Dr. Phil airs clips from SUWS of the Carolinas and Aspen Ranch. Retrieved January 6, 2006 from http://www.aspeneducation.com/drphilsuwsnc.html

Mossman, E., & Goldthorpe, C. (2004). Adventure development counselling research study: Some "hows" and "whys" of doing research. In S. Bandoroff and S. Newes (Eds.), *Coming of age: The evolving field of adventure therapy* (pp. 156–171). Boulder, CO: Association for Experiential Education.

Neill, J. T. (2002, January). *Meta-analytic research on the outcomes of outdoor education.* Paper presented at the 6th Biennial Coalition for Education in the Outdoors Research Symposium, Bradford Woods, IN.

Neill, J. T. (2003). Reviewing and benchmarking adventure therapy outcomes: Applications of meta-analysis. *Journal of Experiential Education, 25*, 316–321.

Neuman, W. L. (1997). *Social research methods: Qualitative and quantitative approaches* (3rd Ed.). Needham Heights, MA: Allyn & Bacon.

Newes, S. (2001). Future directions in adventure-based therapy research: Methodological considerations and design suggestions. *Journal of Experiential Education, 24(2)*, 92–99.

Patton, M. Q. (1987). *How to use qualitative methods in evaluation.* Beverly Hills, CA: Sage.

Romi, S., & Kohan, E. (2004). Wilderness programs: Principles, possibilities and opportunities for intervention with dropout adolescents. *Child & Youth Care Forum, 33*, 115–136

Russell, K. C. (2003). Assessing treatment outcomes in outdoor behavioral healthcare using the Youth Outcome Questionnaire. *Child and Youth Care Forum, 32*, 355–381.

Russell, K. C. (2004). Research directions in wilderness therapy. In S. Bandoroff and S. Newes (Eds.), *Coming of age: The evolving field of adventure therapy* (pp. 137–155). Boulder, CO: Association for Experiential Education.

Russell, K. C. (2005). Two years later: A qualitative assessment of youth well-being and the role of aftercare in outdoor behavioral healthcare treatment. *Child and Youth Care Forum, 34*, 209–239.

Russell, K. C. (2006). Evaluating the effects of the Wendigo Lake expedition program on young offenders. *Youth Violence and Juvenile Justice, 4(2)*, 185–203.

Russell, K., & Sibthorp, J. (2004). Hierarchical data structures in adventure education and therapy. *Journal of Experiential Education, 27,* 176–190.

Sackett, D. L., Rosenberg, W. M., Gray, J. A. M., Haynes, R. B., & Richardson, W. S. (1996). Evidence based medicine: What it is and what it isn't. *British Medical Journal, 312,* 71 – 72.

Sugarman, D. (2005). "I am more than my cancer:" An exploratory examination of adventure programming and cancer survivors. *Journal of Experiential Education, 28,* 72–83.

Voruganti, L., Whatham, J., Bard, E., Parker, G., Babbey, C., Ryan, J., et al. (2006). Going beyond: An adventure and recreation-based group intervention promotes well-being and weight loss in schizophrenia. *Canadian Journal of Psychiatry, 51*(9), 575–580.

CHAPTER 7

Overview of
Specific Programs

A rmed with the information presented in the first six chapters of this book, you are now ready to embark on the process of researching specific programs. In order to help you begin that process, we now present information about the variety of programs that are available, as well as specifics about some prominent programs that utilize the outdoor environment as part of their treatment. Whenever possible, we discuss the philosophical and theoretical ideas from which a program's design are drawn. We also present information on the location and type of programming offered, the level of family participation, program and staff credentials, and cost. As previously mentioned, programs often fall into more than one of the three categories pertinent to this book (wilderness therapy programs, court-related programs, and residential programs). As a result, we also briefly describe some court-related programs and some more traditional residential programs for adolescents that make use of the wilderness environment in their treatment.

The programs we present are a small sample of available options in the United States. For example, the expedition-type wilderness therapy programs we describe are those that currently are members of the Outdoor Behavioral Healthcare Industry Council (OBHIC). These programs are usually nonresidential, which means that participants return home after completion of the program. The court-related and residential programs we list are accredited by the Association for Experiential Education. There are certainly a number of fine programs that fit into these categories that are not included in this chapter. It is the intent of this chapter to provide enough information to encourage more indepth exploration of these and other wilderness therapy programs.

Because the Internet is most people's starting point for research, we laid the groundwork for this chapter by examining program websites in order to see what information is initially presented to the public. The quality and depth of information presented on websites varied greatly, with some programs providing very comprehensive information, while others supplied very little. In all cases, however, the sites identified ways to contact them for more information, usually by phone or e-mail. We followed up Internet research with phone calls or e-mail correspondence and recommend you do the same. (To facilitate the research process, we provide website addresses and phone numbers as starting points for gathering additional information.)

Before discussing programs individually, we want to briefly comment on the dimensions on which we have compared them. There are a variety of types of programs that use the wilderness, each founded on unique philosophies and approaches. Often, the philosophical ideas underlying a program dictate how it operates. For example, some programs have a religious foundation. In these programs, students are often taught to view the wilderness in a reverent way. Other programs are based in a strong affinity for nature. Sometimes these programs utilize Native American teachings and practices.

All of the programs offer support for families and view families as integral to the treatment process. Involvement of families varies, however. Some programs require only short meetings with families, while others require that family members attend workshops and/or meet on the trail at the end of the program.

Staff credentials and availability are important yet difficult issues to highlight. Most programs provide information about the credentials of their current staff rather than stating the degree requirements for each position. Thus, with staff turnover, it is difficult to assess what credentials the staff possesses on an ongoing basis. It is best to contact the program directly for current information. We believe that clinical staff providing therapy services should have graduate degrees in a mental health discipline like psychology, social work, or counseling, and that these therapists should be fully licensed in the state in which they practice. Programs vary on the amount of contact that participants have with the clinical staff. Most use field staff without advanced degrees to interact with participants on a daily basis. Then, clinical staff meet the participants once or twice a week. A few programs include clinical staff on the trip with the participants, giving them daily access to therapy.

As discussed in Chapter 5, licensure and accreditation are critical in evaluating wilderness programs, and these credentials vary widely among programs. Programs with schools are usually accredited by their state educational accrediting agency. For more about state regulation, accreditation, individual licensing, and professional organization affiliations, see Chapter 5.

Finally, issues of cost are critical to consider. Program costs vary widely depending on the type of program selected, the length of the program, and the funding source for the program. Many wilderness programs require a certain minimum number of days in the program and base the actual length of participation on the progress of the participant. Parents can easily expect to pay up to $30,000 for an expedition-type program. Court-related programs are more likely to be at least partially subsidized by the state, thus reducing the cost to families. And residential and hospital-based programs are the most likely to be reimbursed. As previously mentioned, OBHIC programs have taken a leadership role in trying to secure insurance reimbursement for wilderness programs. At this time, however, health insurance companies have not reliably paid for wilderness programs. Families therefore must self-pay, with most programs offering assistance with securing loans.

We now turn to a description of three types of wilderness treatment programs, as well as details about some specific programs. The inclusion of programs in this chapter does not represent an endorsement. Conversely, if a program is not featured, that is no reflection on our assessment of its quality.

Basic Structure of Wilderness Therapy Programs

A number of wilderness therapy programs have been developed throughout the country, with the vast majority of these programs catering to troubled youth experiencing mental health and/or behavioral symptoms. As previously discussed, wilderness therapy programs are different than programs that are called therapeutic. Wilderness therapy involves the use of traditional therapy techniques, especially group techniques, in outdoor settings, sometimes using adventure-based activities as adjuncts to therapy. Wilderness therapy is a carefully planned and methodical treatment. All of the potential respondents should be screened for admission and receive an in-depth clinical evaluation. Ideally, all services should be provided by staff who are fully licensed and credentialed (Davis-Berman & Berman, 1994).

Not surprisingly, many wilderness therapy programs are privately sponsored, with some for-profit and some nonprofit offerings. Some wilderness therapy programs are connected to an inpatient mental health facility, while others have a residential component. Participants typically live at the program site for a period of time and go on wilderness trips or excursions as part of their treatment. The programs that are more residential in nature usually offer some kind of educational component for participants, allowing them to keep up in school. Still others are exclusively expedition-style programs, where participants return immediately after the conclusion of the program to their home communities. Due to the widespread problem of substance abuse in young people, many of the wilderness therapy programs serve adolescents with dual diagnoses, usually including one mental health and one substance abuse diagnosis.

Wilderness therapy programs serve participants with a variety of mental health and behavioral problems. Diagnoses such as depression, anxiety, attention deficit disorder (ADD), attention deficit disorder with hyperactivity (ADHD), and oppositional defiant disorder (ODD) are common among the adolescents in these programs. Adolescents who have problems with self-esteem and anger control are also frequently served in these programs. In addition, many participants are chemically dependent. Sometimes programs list conditions that exclude the participation of chemically dependent individuals up front, while others make these decisions on a case-by-case basis during the admissions process. This is an important issue to consider when determining if an adolescent's needs can be met by a particular program.

In terms of therapy, the approaches reported are as diverse as the clients served and the program designs. However, wilderness therapy programs that emphasize substance abuse treatment primarily use the "12 Step" approach or some variation of this model (based on the philosophies of both Alcoholics Anonymous and Al-Anon). All of the wilderness therapy programs mention individual and/or group therapy approaches. Often the availability of therapy is mentioned, yet specifics as to the frequency or type of approach used usually are not discussed.

In wilderness therapy programs, a combination of group and individual psychotherapy is optimal. Group therapy is usually a central feature of wilderness therapy programs. These sessions are in addition to the daily group meetings that deal with the everyday issues and conflicts arising on the trip. Group therapy is a planned process that is based on the treatment plans and issues of each participant. Ideally, group therapy should be provided by a licensed therapist.

Often, individual therapy is offered on an as-needed basis, and this work can occur informally. For example, in our Wilderness Therapy Program, it is not unusual for individual therapy to occur while walking down the trail. Therapy services should be based on individual treatment plans and should be provided by licensed therapists.

Wilderness therapy programs generally charge participants a per-diem fee for the program. Some specify a minimum number of days that participants must remain in the program, while others are more open ended, and the length of the program depends on the assessment by the program staff that the participant is ready to leave. Importantly, all of the wilderness therapy programs profiled in this chapter report offering a variety of payment options, have staff to assist parents in applying for educational loans, and say that health insurance may cover part or all of the costs. That said, the difficulty in accessing insurance benefits for wilderness therapy programs has prevented many families from using these programs. Although there are some programs that receive state funding; the majority do not. As a result, most participants of wilderness therapy programs must use private funds.

Health insurance coverage for residential treatment varies greatly depending on the health insurance policy. Wilderness therapy programs are often considered to be residential in nature because the treatment occurs outside of the home community. This may apply even to expedition programs, where the participants are on extended expedition, then return home. Insurance coverage is based on medical necessity, and it is up to the health insurance company to determine if the requested level of service is necessary. The determination of the appropriate level of care for an adolescent will most likely be made via the telephone by a clinician employed by the insurance company. It is important to inquire about coverage early in the process of selecting a wilderness therapy program, as determination of eligibility often requires a substantial amount of time and effort.

In order to provide a more realistic feel for some of these wilderness therapy programs, brief descriptions of some representative programs are given. Bear in mind that this information may change after publication.

Expeditionary Wilderness Therapy Programs

As we send this book to the printer, all of the expedition-type wilderness therapy programs profiled are current members of the OBHIC and include: Anasazi, The Aspen Achievement Academy, Catherine Freer Wilderness Therapy Programs, Monarch Center for Family Healing, Mountain Homes Youth Ranch, OMNI Youth Services, Phoenix Outdoor, Red-Cliff Ascent, School of Urban and Wilderness Survival, Soltreks, Three Rivers Montana, and Wilderness Quest. Most of these programs involve expeditions of some sort, returning the participants to home following completion of the program. We call these expedition-type wilderness therapy programs to distinguish them from the residential programs that include a wilderness therapy component.

Anasazi

Based in Arizona, Anasazi offers programs for males and females aged 12 to 17, and young adults aged 18 to 25. First developed in 1988, the youth program is specifically geared toward adolescents with substance abuse and emotional/behavioral problems. This program is very direct in presenting its policy about psychiatric medication. It states that it will only take teens who do not need to have blood work done to monitor their medications. It also excludes participants whose medication affects hydration, appetite, or mental or emotional attentiveness. These exclusions are in effect to avoid the dangers of dehydration. Also, medications that are extremely sedating can adversely affect the participant taking the medications, thus disrupting the entire group experience. Anasazi is unusual in this exclusionary policy.

This program, although not directly based in religion, is founded on a reverence for God and nature as created by God. It teaches using a "primitive lifestyle," an approach that is nature based and involves developing a comfort with living in the natural world without using "contrived experiences." Fire-building and other ancient skills are taught, with the goal being self-sufficiency in the wilderness environment. Participants are given essential equipment, and they learn how to construct shelters for themselves. Although it teaches basic skills, Anasazi is not a survivalist program, and participants are not deprived of anything they might need to safely exist in the wilderness.

The main mode of experiencing the wilderness in this program is hiking, with participants often covering up to 10 miles per day. In addition to learning trust and cooperation, participants are provided with both individual and group therapy by clinical staff on a weekly basis on the trail.

Parents are a critical part of this program and must be involved in an orientation and a relationship seminar. Family counseling also occurs on a weekly basis, either in person or by phone. At the end of the program, parents and adolescent are reunited through a final walk, during which they spend two nights and three days on the trail together.

In addition to being a member of OBHIC, Anasazi is a member of NATSAP and is licensed by the Arizona Department of Health Service and accredited by The Joint Commission and COA.

The staff-to-participant ratio is one staff member for every three participants. All of the adolescents are assigned a counselor (called a shadow). This counselor has at least a master's degree and is supervised by the psychologist or clinical director. The clinical staff all have appropriate degrees in mental health. The therapists provide weekly individual and group therapy services on the trail for the participants. They are not, however, on the trail with the participants on a daily basis.

The daily cost of the Anasazi program is approximately $435. This does not include transportation to and from the site or a physical examination prior to the start of the program. Partial scholarships may be available, and parents are assisted with securing loans. Some health insurance companies may also provide some coverage. There is a 42-day minimum stay in the program, reflecting a minimum cost of $18,270. If a youth is in the program longer than the 42-day minimum, the extra days are billed at a reduced rate.

Website: www.anasazi.org ▪ **Phone**: 800-678-3445

Aspen Achievement Academy

Located in the state of Utah, Aspen Achievement Academy specializes in treating boys and girls aged 13 to 18 who experience low self-esteem, low motivation, depression, school problems, substance abuse, or oppositional and defiant behaviors. Although the length of the program varies, there is a 35-day minimum. Aspen describes itself as a "licensed treatment program that integrates an accredited academic component, a sophisticated therapeutic model, and an experiential education curriculum in a healing wilderness environment" (www.aspenacademy.com). A long list of admission exclusions is made available by this program and includes such conditions as: severe depression, acute suicide risk, history of violence or sexual abuse, and mental retardation. Participants with eating disorders, diabetes, and epilepsy might also be excluded from participating.

This program consists of four phases: (1) Mouse—entry-level participants dealing with being placed in the program, (2) Coyote—a time to focus on character development and the good of the community, (3) Buffalo—dealing with group responsibility and accountability, and (4) Eagle—becoming self-reliant and a leader. Within this framework, the program provides individual, family, and group therapy, as well as recreation and experiential activities and an educational component. *Aspen Achievement Academy* was the setting for the book *Shouting at the Sky* (Ferguson, 1999), profiled in Chapter 4, which provides an in-depth look at the day-by-day operations of a wilderness therapy program.

Parent participation is considered critical to the success of this program. As such, parents are required to attend a two-and-a-half-day workshop at the end of the program, and are expected to participate in family therapy sessions as needed. A family reunion is conducted at the end of the program, during which participants meet their family members on the trail. This phase of the program can also include family therapy and parent workshops.

In addition to being a member of OBHIC, the Aspen Achievement Academy is a member of NATSAP, is accredited by The Joint Commission, and is licensed as an outdoor treatment program through the Utah Department of Human Services.

This is a large program, employing field and clinical staff. The clinical staff all have appropriate degrees in mental health. They meet the participants on the trail at least twice a week and sometimes stay overnight on the trail.

The program charges approximately $440/day and requires a minimum stay of 35 days. Program data suggests that the average stay is 49 days. If this average stay is exceeded, the daily rate from that point drops somewhat. Thus, the minimum cost for this program is $15,400, with the average cost being $21,560. The program offers assistance with securing loans and provides a discounted rate for participants who are private pay. Some insurance reimbursement might also be possible

Website: www.aspenacademy.com ▪ **Phone**: 800-283-8334

Catherine Freer Wilderness Therapy Programs

Located in Oregon, the Catherine Freer program has been in business since 1988. This expedition program serves boys and girls aged 13 to 18, and offers either 21- or 51-day treks. Catherine Freer's expedition program treats participants with the following problems: school problems, substance abuse, ADD, ADHD, family problems, depression, emotional problems, and anger and defiance. The program lists a number of criteria that exclude potential participants. These include: serious suicide risk, violence, need for ongoing medical supervision, diabetes, IV drug use, need for drug detox, and some medications. The 21-day program uses a 12-Step approach to working with drug and behavioral problems, and participants take part in both individual and group therapy. The 51-day program is an extension of the shorter program and is designed for participants who need more time in treatment and have successfully completed the first phase.

While it does not have a residential component affiliated with its mental health program, it does have a therapeutic school program called Santiam Crossing, which integrates wilderness, education, service, and treatment. In this residential program, there is an emphasis on academics. In order to be considered for admission to Santiam Crossing, an adolescent must have successfully completed the traditional 51-day expedition program. The minimum stay in the Santiam Crossing program is 3 months, with an average of 6 to 9 months.

Parents are encouraged to be involved in their child's treatment, and are required to attend an all-day multifamily meeting at the beginning and end of each expedition. During these meetings, parents receive information about the program, as well as support from other parents and suggestions for making changes at home. Parents also are sent written updates about their child during the trek.

All of the therapists in this program possess either master's or doctoral degrees in psychology or social work. A therapist and a drug counselor accompany the participants on the trip at all times. Thus, group and individual therapy is available on a 24-hour basis if needed. The constant presence of therapists on the trail with participants distinguishes this program from others.

The director of the Catherine Freer program has a Ph.D. in psychology and has been awarded the Industry Leadership Award by the National Association of Therapeutic Schools and Programs. The clinical staff all have appropriate degrees in mental health. In addition to being a member of OBHIC and NATSAP, the Catherine Freer program is licensed by the state of Oregon as a residential substance abuse treatment and mental health day treatment program for adolescents and is accredited by The Joint Commission. In 2002, ABC Primetime aired a documentary about six adolescents participating in the 21-day program.

Rather than charging on a per-diem basis, this program charges a fee for the entire program. The charge for the 21-day program is $9,845. There is a $500 equipment charge. The fee for the 51-day program, is approximately $23,195. Due to the 24-hour availability of therapy services, insurance reimbursements may be possible with this program. This is because this level of staffing is more consistent with a traditional residential treatment program. Loan assistance is also available.

Website: www.cfreer.com ▪ **Phone**: 800-390-3983

Monarch Center for Family Healing

When the Monarch Program first opened in 1996, it was called the Trailhead Wilderness School and was the first licensed outdoor residential childcare facility in the state of Colorado. Originally, this program received referrals from the state. In 2005, due to state budget constraints, Trailhead Wilderness School closed for a few months, then reopened as the Monarch Center for Family Healing, and has since served private-pay families.

This program offers a long-term wilderness therapy program. It states that its program is open to male and female adolescents aged 10 to

18 experiencing problems such as depression, ADD, ADHD, substance abuse, anger control problems, grief reactions, suicidal thinking, and a host of other issues.

Both individual and group therapy are provided on the trail by the therapists of the program. The Monarch Center states that its programming is based on the following three philosophies: wilderness therapy, Gestalt therapy, and family therapy.

Family involvement is considered of paramount importance at Monarch. Families participate in meetings called "family intensives." They also must participate in regular family therapy meetings. Finally, family members may sometimes join their adolescent on the trail in the backcountry.

This family-owned program was cofounded by Dave and Lori Ventimiglia. The Ventimiglias are still in charge of the program today and serve as its executive directors. The clinical staff members have appropriate degrees in mental health disciplines. Although the frequency of therapy is not completely clear, the therapists join the group on the trail to provide individual and group therapy. They are generally in the field 2 days a week.

In addition to maintaining memberships with OBHIC, NATSAP, NATWC, and AEE, Monarch is licensed as a residential childcare facility and children's camp in Colorado.

The daily cost of this program is approximately $395, with an additional one-time equipment fee of $750. Participants are required to spend a minimum of 30 days in the program, with stays averaging 60 to 80 days. Assuming a participant will be in the program the average number of days, the minimum cost would be $23,700, and the maximum cost would be $31,600.

Website: www.monarchfamilyhealing.com ▪ Phone: 303-569-0767

Mountain Homes Youth Ranch

Located in the state of Colorado, this expeditionary program serves male and female adolescents between the ages of 12 and 17, and is run from a working cattle ranch. The program also has a residential component if needed. Due to the length of the programs (84 or 105 days), participants can earn academic credit while at the ranch. Participants are generally struggling with issues such as ADD, ADHD, depression, Tourette's syndrome, bipolar disorder, conduct disorder, and anxiety.

There are three phases of the program: beginning, advanced, and ranch. During the beginning phase, the focus is on developing basic wilderness skills and self-awareness. During the advanced phase, participants work on developing a sense of community and interdependence. Finally, the ranch phase focuses on integrating participants back into society and establishing communication with parents and other family members.

Parents are involved from the beginning of the program, at which time they are asked to provide input to the therapist during the development of the treatment plan. Parents are also encouraged to communicate with the treatment team throughout the duration of the program. During the ranch phase of the program, participants learn how to better communicate with their parents. At the conclusion of the program, parents attend a graduation and spend some time on the ranch with their child.

The clinical director and clinical staff possess graduate degrees in appropriate mental health disciplines. Therapists provide therapy to the participants once a week on the trail (Caldwell, 2006). The treatment team meets weekly and encourages input from parents.

In addition to membership in OBHIC and NATSAP, this facility is licensed by the state of Colorado as a residential childcare facility. It is also occasionally featured on the *Dr. Phil* show as a treatment center to which they refer troubled adolescents.

The cost of the program is approximately $325 per day with an 84-day minimum stay, making the minimum tuition $27,300. The outfitting fee is $750 in winter and $500 in summer. Insurance reimbursement may be possible based on the medical necessity for residential treatment.

Website: www.mhyr.com ▪ **Phone**: 866-781-2450

OMNI Youth Services

OMNI Youth Services is a comprehensive youth and family social service agency. Established in 1972, OMNI now serves more than 15,000 male and female youth and adolescents in 19 communities in the Northwest suburbs of Chicago. Experiential approaches are valued at this agency and are infused into all OMNI programs.

One of the specialty services OMNI offers to appropriate adolescents is an expedition-type wilderness therapy program. These expedition experiences range from 1 to 10 days and provide a variety of outdoor and wilderness experiences, from 1-day ropes courses to extended backpacking trips.

OMNI is noteworthy in that all the clinical staff present on these expeditions have graduate degrees in mental health. Additionally, they are on the trip with participants at all times. This level of professional staffing distinguishes this program from many others.

In addition to being a member of OBHIC and AEE, OMNI is accredited by COA.

Due to state/federal partnership cost sharing, the per-diem charge for families for the wilderness expedition is between $50 and $65. Obviously, due its restricted area of service, OMNI isn't an option for all adolescents. **Website:** www.omniyouth.org ▪ **Phone:** 847-353-1774

Phoenix Outdoor

Based in Asheville, North Carolina, Phoenix Outdoor is part of the Aspen Education Group and serves males and females aged 13 to 17 who are experiencing substance abuse and chemical dependency, and mental health and behavioral problems. The program is structured on a repeating cycle so that participants spend 5 days backpacking, then return to base camp for 2 days. Treatment is based on individualized treatment plans and a 12-Step model, if appropriate.

Each family is assigned a team of two therapists. Families participates in weekly telephone sessions with their therapists. Parents also have access to weekly reports, pictures, and updates on their child's progress via the Internet.

The clinical staff of the program all possess appropriate graduate degrees in mental health.

Phoenix Outdoor is a member of OBHIC and is licensed by the state of North Carolina Department of Health and Human Services as a therapeutic camp.

The per-diem rate for services is $ 455, and stays average 6 to 8 weeks, so the average cost ranges from $19,110 to $25,480.
Website: www.phoenixoutdoor.com ▪ **Phone:** 877-305-0904 or 888-868-8233.

RedCliff Ascent

Founded in 1993 and located in southern Utah, RedCliff Ascent serves boys and girls between the ages of 13 and 17. Participants are usually in the program between 45 and 60 days. It also offers a program called Medicine Wheel for young adults aged 18 to 25. Typical problems addressed in this program include: depression, bipolar disorder, ADD, ADHD, ODD, learning disabilities, adjustment disorders, impulse control problems, and substance abuse. The program lists some exclusionary criteria such as: a weight of less than 90 pounds, diabetes, autism, epilepsy, severe asthma or allergies, and active hallucinations. All applicants must pass a physical, and those taking psychiatric medications must be approved by the clinical director.

This program states that it offers the same level of treatment as traditional residential programs and that the main differences are the length of the program and the use of the wilderness environment. RedCliff Ascent believes that the wilderness setting and the challenge of the program allow it to offer residential-like services in a few months, whereas traditional programs last from 6 to 12 months. The program does not utilize a survival-ist philosophy, and one of it goals is to facilitate a sense of equity between staff and participants. Thus, on the trail all are viewed as equals, eating the same food and sleeping in the same type of shelter.

Prior to the trip, staff elicits relevant information from parents. During the trek, parents are encouraged to write to their child. Therapists also talk to the parents by phone on a weekly basis. The end of the trip involves a parent-child reunion on the trail. Participants actually complete a 2-mile run and end that run meeting their parents on the trail. This ritual often is a meaningful and emotional time, signaling the beginning of a new dynamic in the family.

The clinical staff have appropriate degrees in mental health. Each adolescent is assigned a therapist who provides weekly individual and group therapy. A treatment team reviews each case weekly with the clinical director.

In addition to maintaining memberships with OBHIC and NAT-SAP, this program is licensed as a treatment provider by the state of Utah.

RedCliff Ascent was the host of the original *Brat Camp* filming when adolescent participants from the United Kingdom were followed and filmed in the program in Utah. This film was aired in the United Kingdom, Australia, and on the ABC Family Channel in the United States (Jones, 2005). Refer back to Chapter 3 for a comprehensive discussion of *Brat Camp*. RedCliff Ascent was also featured in the United States during the summer of 2006 in a documentary film on wilderness therapy (*Teen Wilderness Camps: Therapy or Punishment?*).

The cost of RedCliff Ascent is approximately $440 per day, for a total of $13,200 for the first 30 days. There is an extra charge of $500 for clothing. After 60 days in the program, the per diem fee is reduced to $220. The average participant stays between 45 and 60 days. The program suggests that parents attempt to obtain insurance coverage or ask for assistance with loans.

Website: www.redcliffascent.com ▪ **Phone:** 800-898-1244

School of Urban and Wilderness Survival Wilderness Programs

Developed in 1981, the School of Urban and Wilderness Survival (SUWS) was the first licensed outdoor program in the state of Idaho. At its inception, it was a survival school. Now, as a program owned by the Aspen Education Group, its emphasis has changed to growth and therapy. SUWS has programs for male and female adolescents, lasting between four and nine weeks, and one for younger boys and girls.

The adolescent program serves participants who are experiencing problems such as ADD, ADHD, anxiety, mood disorders, attachment disorders, and low self-esteem. The program lists a number of exclusionary criteria including: antisocial personality disorder, dissociative disorder, extreme suicide risk, violence, severe depression, severe eating disorders, and serious self-mutilation. One of the stated goals of the program is to assist adolescents in focusing on inner strength by learning to function effectively on a team. The program is divided into eight stages designed to facilitate that process. These are:

1. Orientation, which focuses on safety and assessment
2. Individual, which focuses on awareness and identity
3. Family, which focuses on interpersonal relationships
4. Venturer, which focuses on teamwork and service
5. Explorer, which focuses on self-reflection
6. Navigator, which focuses on goal development
7. Guide, which teaches leadership
8. Search and Rescue, which focuses on giving back and future pacing

A solo experience is also required of all participants.

SUWS encourages parental involvement through a number of mechanisms. There is the parent extranet program, which enables parents to access their child's personal website 3 days after the adolescent has begun to participate. Here, parents can receive updates on their child's progress and view pictures. Parents are also encouraged to meet with program supervisors throughout their child's involvement with the program, and a parent-supervisor meeting near the end of the program is devoted to planning family participation in the graduation segment of the program.

Each trip has two field instructors who are on the trail on a full-time basis. All of the therapists in the program have appropriate graduate degrees in mental health disciplines.

In addition to being a member of OBHIC, SUWS was the first outdoor treatment center licensed in the state of Idaho.

The daily rate is approximately $440, making the total range from a low of $13,200 to a high of $29,480. There is also a $1,000 enrollment fee. Individuals are encouraged to contact the program for information about financing, including student loans.

Website: www.suws.com ▪ **Phone:** 888-879-7897

Soltreks

Established in 1997, the Soltreks program is located in Minnesota and offers some unique options for families. One such program is Soltreks' personalized, private treks that last a minimum of 30 days. This involves the pairing of a male or female adolescent with an adventure-based counselor. While the private trek offers the opportunity to experience the wilderness environment, it lacks the ability to help adolescents work on leadership skills and working and living in community with others.

Soltreks also offers more traditional programs like the other wilderness therapy programs we've discussed. Winter and summer group programs are run for male and female adolescents between the ages of 13 and 17. The summer program is designed to be about 6 weeks in length, and the winter program varies between 4 and 8 weeks. Typically, participants are struggling with issues such as ADD, ADHD, low self-esteem, problems with peer relationships, boundary issues, and substance abuse.

Soltreks believes that parental involvement is critical to the success of its program. As such, parents are included in the initial program orientation, and they are given assignments to complete that relate to their child's treatment. They are also encouraged to write letters to their child throughout treatment. Parents are then privy to a midtrek assessment of their child's progress. Finally, the graduation involves a family session. Families can elect to participate in a family trek, lasting usually between 4 and 7 days.

The executive director of the Soltreks program is also its cofounder. The clinical staff have appropriate degrees in a mental health discipline.

Soltreks maintains memberships with OBHIC, NATSAP, NATWC, and AEE.

The cost of the program is approximately $420 per day. Although trips can be of varied length, the usual minimum is 30 days, making the cost $12,600. Individualized treks are more expensive.

Website: www.soltreks.com   ▪   **Phone**: 218-834-4607

Three Rivers Montana

Located in Montana, this program serves males and females aged 13 to 18 who are experiencing a variety of emotional and behavioral problems at school and home. This program is unique in that with the completion of assignments, participants can earn 6 high-school credits. It also offers 3 months of intensive aftercare services for no additional charge to families if the adolescent returns home after the program. Also, this program encourages participants to explore spirituality in a nondenominational way.

Participants begin at base camp, then go on extended wilderness expeditions. The therapists join the participants in the field and provide therapy there. Therapists are in the field at least two days and one night per week.

Initially, parents attend a 2-day workshop. They are encouraged to communicate with the therapists throughout the program and are also sent letters from their adolescent. Finally, parents are invited to camp at base camp as their adolescent completes the program.

All of the clinical staff have appropriate graduate degrees in mental health disciplines. Therapy is provided both at base camp and in the field.

Three Rivers Montana maintains memberships with OBHIC, NATSAP, and AEE.

The per-diem rate is $450, with average stays ranging 6 to 9 weeks, bringing the average cost of participation from $18,900 to $28,350.
Website: www.threeriversmontana.org ▪ **Phone:** 877-221-1115

Wilderness Quest

Located in the state of Utah, this program has been in operation for 34 years, and serves male and female adolescents aged 14 to 17 and young adults aged 18 to 28. The program specializes in the treatment of substance abuse, yet it also serves participants with behavioral and mental health problems. Some of the problems typically experienced by participants include depression, anxiety, low self-esteem, oppositional disorder, and self-destructive tendencies. This program is based on the 12-Step model and does not utilize punitive techniques to facilitate change or as consequences for behavior.

Parents are an important part of the treatment and are required to attend a family workshop at the conclusion of the program. Families also are required to work on a specialized curriculum that corresponds to the content of the wilderness program. In addition, families participate in weekly phone consultations and updates with the clinical staff about the participant's progress. Parents are also involved with follow-up on a monthly basis after their child is discharged from the program.

The administrative and clinical staff of this program possess appropriate graduate degrees in mental health. During the program, professional staff are available at all times, with one therapist and one chemical dependency counselor on each team at all times. This kind of full-time availability of the clinical staff is unusual and impressive among wilderness therapy programs.

In addition to membership in OBHIC, Wilderness Quest is accredited by The Joint Commission and the National Association of Alcoholism and Drug Abuse Counselors (NAADAC). It is also licensed as an adolescent/family wilderness therapy program by the state of Utah.

The daily tuition cost of the program is approximately $460. Although a minimum number of days is not clearly specified, participants must pay $23,000 at the beginning of the program, which is equivalent to roughly 50 days of treatment.

Website: www.wildernessquest.com ▪ **Phone**: 888-929-2225

Court-Related Wilderness Programs

Although a number of the expedition-type wilderness therapy programs incorporate clients with court-related issues, there are some wilderness programs devoted strictly to the treatment of delinquents. Many participants in these programs suffer from addictions or psychological problems or, more commonly, both.

The severity of the difficulties experienced by delinquent clients truly distinguishes these court-related programs from other mental health programs. Adolescents sent to these programs often have been in numerous outpatient and inpatient settings, where they have failed to change in meaningful ways. Thus, wilderness programs for delinquents usually serve as an alternative to traditional incarceration or as an adjunct to some kind of residential care. In such situations, wilderness trips are based and run out of a residential program to which the clients return upon completion of the wilderness experience. Court-related programs tend to be highly structured, regulated, and supervised.

Similar to the wilderness therapy expedition-type programs, court-related programs are funded in a number of ways, including some interesting public/private joint programs. Many court-related programs are funded by the state and federal government, meaning participants are not required to pay. How programs use wilderness experiences also varies greatly between programs, with offerings ranging from ropes courses of only one day's duration to lengthy camping and expedition programs in wilderness environments. Some programs are restricted to a small geographic area, and are supported and funded by local or state department of corrections, while others serve a geographically diverse clientele.

As with the wilderness therapy expedition-type programs, the following section does not attempt to describe all or even a representative number of court-related wilderness programs. Our aim is to give the reader a feel for the kinds of programs that are available. The programs briefly discussed below include Camp Woodson, Eckerd Youth Alternative programs, the Santa Fe Mountain Center, and VisionQuest.

Camp Woodson

Founded in 1976, Camp Woodson offers a short-term, voluntary pre-release program for incarcerated adolescents in North Carolina that provides a transitionary step between incarceration and home. Even though participation is limited to North Carolina residents, we mention this program because it represents a rather innovative court-based wilderness program.

Woodson focuses on developing personal responsibility and group cooperation by exposing delinquents to outdoor adventure experiences in which they can experience success. Through the use of activities such as white-water canoeing and backpacking, the wilderness environment is used as a place to teach natural consequences. Efforts are made to apply these lessons to the transition to home.

The field staff have undergraduate degrees in social science disciplines, while the clinical supervisor has a graduate degree in an appropriate mental health discipline. Because this program is operated by the state of North Carolina, it is offered at no charge to families (Silver, 2006). **Website:** www.ncdjjdp.org ▪ **Phone:** 828-686-9595

Eckerd Youth Alternatives

The Eckerd Youth Alternative program is a large multifaceted organization that was founded in Florida in 1968. Today, the Eckerd program is nationally known for its specialized programs for juvenile offenders, which were some of the first to be privatized. It also runs a number of general programs in various states including Ohio, Tennessee, North Carolina, Georgia, Florida, Rhode Island, Vermont, and New Hampshire. The Eckerd program philosophy is based in a belief in God and focuses on the uniqueness of each young person. The goal is to help participants develop a balance between their physical, intellectual, emotional, and spiritual selves.

Eckerd is a private, nonprofit agency that serves youth and adolescents between the ages of 8 and 18 who are at risk for behavioral problems. In order to qualify for admission, youth must have an IQ of at least 75 and must be able to understand cause and effect. The Eckerd program offers both non-secure and secure residential treatment facilities for juvenile delinquents. Its secure residential treatment facility serves both males and females and has been rated in the top 1% in the country by the American Correctional Association. Eckerd's large number of offerings range from day programs to long-term residential treatment. Participants learn about anger management and methods for peacefully resolving conflict. Due to the sheer number of programs and participants served, interested parties should contact centers directly.

Similarly, staffing varies a great deal, based on the programs that are offered. For example, the programs in Florida, Georgia, New Hampshire, North Carolina, Rhode Island, Tennessee, and Vermont are all accredited by COA and the Southern Association of Schools and Colleges. The programs in Ohio are accredited by the Association of Child Caring Agencies. The entire Eckerd organization is a member of NATSAP and NATWC. In order to determine the program and staff credentials for each program, the Eckerd program should be contacted directly.

It is impossible to provide general information about the costs of Eckerd programs due to the variety of offerings and the types of funding partnerships that exist. Some of the programs require families to pay. Others include the possibility of insurance reimbursement. Finally, some are funded by the state in which they operate and are offered at no cost to families.
Website: www.eckerd.org ▪ **Phone**: 800-914-3937

Santa Fe Mountain Center

Based primarily in New Mexico, the Santa Fe Mountain Center has been a leader in the innovative treatment of delinquents for the past 25 years. This program is coed, private, nonprofit, and offers alternatives ranging from 1-day team-building experiences to multiday outdoor experiences.

Santa Fe Mountain Center offers a number of programs, including some for Native American youth and other options for at-risk youth. The center also provides extensive community training, as well as education for professionals in the outdoor adventure field. The programs for at-risk youth target those beginning to become involved in drugs, gangs, or violence. There are also programs for adolescents who have entered the juvenile justice system. Many Santa Fe Mountain Center programs are developed and funded in cooperation with state agencies. For example, the youth and family development program is funded by the New Mexico Department of Children, Youth, and Families.

The programs at the Santa Fe Mountain Center are built around an experiential adventure-based resiliency model. This philosophy combines the power of hands-on, experiential learning with aspects of adventure. This approach also focuses on resiliency. The person is considered a whole, and strengths and assets, rather than weaknesses, are stressed.

An example of a court-related wilderness-type program is the Youth Challenge Program. It provides treatment that focuses on accountability for juvenile drug court participants and involves mandatory outdoor activities, including weekend camping trips. Another program that works with clients in the juvenile justice system is the Therapeutic Adventure Program, which uses activities ranging from ropes courses to extensive wilderness experiences. Santa Fe Mountain Center values diversity, and this is reflected in the staff and their qualifications. Some of the staff possess master's degrees, while others do not.

The Santa Fe Mountain Center is accredited by AEE. Additionally, in 2006 it received an award from the New Mexico Human Rights Alliance for the work that it does with gay and lesbian youth and adults.

Due to the wide variety of programs, and the partnering with state and local agencies, it is difficult to make general statements about the costs of all of the programs. For example, with the help of state funding, the Therapeutic Adventure Program is offered at no cost to families (Jevertson, 2006). For specific costs of other programs, the reader is encouraged to contact the program directly.

Website: www.sf-mc.com ▪ **Phone:** 505-983-6158

VisionQuest

Based in Arizona, VisionQuest was founded in 1973 by two Department of Corrections workers who were frustrated with the lack of innovative programming for troubled youth. Participants are referred by state or federal officials to the program, and those who enter a VisionQuest program may choose to participate in a number of different programs, but all must be willing to commit for a period of at least 1 year. In this regard, VisionQuest is a more long-term program than some of the other wilderness therapy or delinquency programs.

VisionQuest has sites in Pennsylvania, Arizona, New Jersey, Florida, Oklahoma, and Delaware, and offers a variety of different programs at these sites, including coed and same-sex residential programs. A central component of all VisionQuest programs is the quest experience. Although the quests differ depending on the particular program, they include instruction in wilderness skills, and a variety of physical and emotional challenges.

As the program's name indicates, there is a strong focus on Native American customs and ceremonies. (As explained on the VisionQuest website, "During a vision quest, Native American adolescents were sent into the wilderness to overcome challenges and discover a view of their futures. VisionQuest seeks to give adjudicated youth this same opportunity to succeed in challenges, see a new future for themselves, and give them skills to accomplish their goals and reach their highest potential.")

A major goal of the VisionQuest program is to integrate the participants with their families following completion of the program. Parents are supported and included in the program whenever possible. Adolescents who have successfully completed one of the VisionQuest programs are eligible to live in a group home setting. This option is open to participants who feel that they are not yet ready to function in their home or community. The goal of this placement is to eventually facilitate the adolescent's adjustment back to that home and community. There is also a HomeQuest program, which serves adolescents living in their local community. Participants come to a VisionQuest facility for their evening meal, activities, and counseling.

Because VisionQuest is such a large program operating in so many states, it is difficult to concisely summarize staff and program credentials, and costs. For example, some VisionQuest residential programs are accredited by The Joint Commission (such as in Pennsylvania), while others are not. Because participants are usually referred by state or federal officials, partial or full assistance with payment is often available. For information about credentialing and costs of specific programs, the reader is encouraged to contact the program directly.

Website: www.vq.com ▪ **Phone:** 610-486-2280 (Eastern office) or 520-881-3950 (Western office)

Residential Programs With Wilderness Components

Programs that are considered to be residential in nature tend to be lengthier and more intensive than expedition-oriented wilderness therapy programs. Often, the adolescents enrolled in residential programs have failed in less restrictive treatment programs and are deemed in need of more in-depth treatment. (See Chapter 1 for a more comprehensive discussion on levels of care in mental health.)

Before considering a residential program, a determination must be made of the adolescent's need for this level of care. Health insurance companies require pre-approval for this type of care. Some residential programs have facilities where adolescents live year round, while others are considered residential because of the extended length of the program. Often, year-round residential programs house participants in a camp setting. Other programs are part of more traditional psychiatric hospitals, and yet others are free-standing residential treatment centers, operating as large ranches. All of the residential programs we discuss below offer a substantial wilderness experience as part of their treatment programs and are examples of wilderness therapy programs within more traditional residential programs. These programs include Inner Harbor Hospitals, Red Top Meadows, Summit Achievement, Wendigo Lake Expeditions, and Wilderness Treatment Center.

Inner Harbour

Developed in 1962 in Georgia, this program serves youth and adolescents between the ages of 6 and 18. Often, these adolescents are suffering from depression, ADD, ADHD, and/or substance addiction. Sometimes, they have failed in less restrictive settings, thus a more structured, longer term placement is needed. Others have demonstrated dysfunctional behaviors in their home communities or have a lack of support in that setting. Program length varies and is usually dependent on the progress of the participant. This program prides itself on its educational component, which is fully accredited by the Southern Association of Colleges and Schools.

Inner Harbour provides a rather extensive experiential therapy department that is made available to all patients throughout the hospital. These techniques are thought to be especially helpful to those for whom traditional approaches have not been effective. Examples of some experiential therapies include art therapy, animal-assisted therapy, equine therapy, therapeutic riding, therapeutic drumming, and ropes course experiences. Two of the programs that utilize experiential therapies include the residential program for adolescents aged 12 to 17 and an adolescent sexual behavior program, serving males between the ages of 12 and 17.

Inner Harbour also sponsors a program for first-time juvenile offenders, called the EXCEL program. Many of the adolescents participate in the educational component of the program. This program seems more traditional than some of the others and relies less on wilderness experiences. Thus, it may be more appealing to adolescents who are reluctant to participate in extensive wilderness experiences.

This facility is accredited by The Joint Commission and is licensed by the state of Georgia as a specialized psychiatric hospital and intensive residential treatment center. It is also accredited by AEE and by the Southern Association of Colleges and Schools.

Staffing and cost depend on the particular program in which the adolescent is involved. Because this is an accredited hospital program, staff credentials are dictated by this accreditation. Also, due to this accreditation, health insurance reimbursement may be more likely. For information on the cost of specific programs, Inner Harbor should be contacted directly. **Website:** www.innerharbour.org ▪ **Phone:** 800-255-8657

Red Top Meadows

Located in Wyoming, Red Top Meadows was developed in 1980. It offers a residential treatment center and a therapeutic wilderness program that is not residential in nature. It also has a residential program, which consists of a private 14-bed, nonprofit program for boys between the ages of 12 and 17. Exclusionary criteria in the residential program include violence that requires restraint, severe developmental issues, the need for detoxification, and a major medical or psychiatric condition that is not currently stabilized.

The residential program includes therapy services, an accredited academic program, wilderness expeditions, gardening, and community service. There is a 1-week wilderness trip in both fall and winter. In spring, a 2-week wilderness trip includes an educational component. The summer trip involves 24 days of backpacking. Red Top Meadows assists participants in working on developing their ability to understand and solve problems, with the aim of successfully integrating back into society. Red Top Meadows also offers an open-enrollment wilderness therapy program in June, during which local agencies or outdoor programs can contract with Red Top to run their wilderness therapy trips.

Family is intensively involved throughout the program, even at admission, during which time they offer valuable assessment information to the staff.

The program director and therapists all have appropriate degrees in mental health disciplines. The program also employs a wilderness program director.

Red Top Meadows is accredited by AEE and the Wyoming Department of Education and the Wyoming Department of Family Services.

Due to the variety of programs offered, it is difficult to provide specific cost information. Tuition is often subsidized by the Department of Family Services if the family qualifies.

Website: www.redtopmeadows.org ▪ **Phone:** 307-733-9098

Summit Achievement

This program has been based in Maine since 1996 and serves adolescents aged 13 to 17 in need of an intensive treatment program. The regular residential program includes four components: weekly individual and daily group therapy, traditional academic instruction, weekly wilderness expeditions, and a residential living setting. Every 3 weeks the therapists go on expedition with the participants for a 48-hour period. In order to successfully complete the program, participants must pass through six levels. Summit Achievement also offers a special program called Summit Semester, which requires a minimum of 60 days of participation.

Parents are involved in the initial development of their adolescent's treatment plan. During the course of the program, parents talk weekly by phone to the therapists. Then, they talk to their child by phone, thus maintaining close contact.

Master's level therapists coordinate and plan all treatment. Also, all of the clinical staff possess appropriate graduate degrees in mental health disciplines.

Summit Achievement is licensed as a residential treatment center with mental health and substance abuse certification in Maine. Its academic program is licensed in the state of Maine as a nontraditional school. It is a member of OBHIC, NATSAP, and AEE.

The per-diem rate is $445, with stays averaging 42 and 56 days, bringing the cost to between $18,690 and $24,920.

Website: www.summitachievement.com ▪ **Phone:** 800-997-8664

Wendigo Lake Expeditions

Based in Ontario, Canada, this program was originally operated by the province of Ontario but became Wendigo Lake Expeditions in 2000. The program for at-risk youth is called the REACH program and serves males aged 14 to 17 experiencing school, family, mental health, and substance abuse problems. Many of the referrals are from state-funded agencies, but private referrals also are welcome. Between 40 and 50 percent of the program takes place on expedition, and the remainder takes place on the main campus.

Parents are encouraged to visit their sons, however these arrangements must be made ahead of time.

All of the clinical staff have graduate degrees in appropriate mental health disciplines.

Wendigo Lake Expeditions is licensed as a residential facility under the Ontario Child and Family Services Act and is accredited by AEE. It also maintains membership with OBHIC and NATSAP.

The per-diem rate for this program is $252 (Canadian), $243 (U.S.). Many of the referrals to this program are subsidized by the Canadian government, thus families do not incur these charges. Private-pay clients are welcome. All participants have been Canadian, however, no rules prohibit the participation of adolescents from other countries. The average length of stay is 4 months, making the private-pay rate $30,202 (Canadian), $29,145 (U.S.).

Website: www.wendigolake.com ▪ Phone: 705-386-2376

Wilderness Treatment Center

Located on a 4,000-acre cattle ranch in Montana, this program is restricted to serving males between the ages of 14 and 24 who are chemically dependent. This is a free-standing treatment center that incorporates residential living with wilderness experiences, all framed within a 12-Step addictions model. This treatment approach is directly tied to Alcoholics Anonymous and Al-Anon. The Wilderness Treatment Center program is unique in that it combines a traditional 30-day residential experience with a 16- to 21-day wilderness therapy expedition. After successfully completing the initial 30-day traditional program, participants are then taken on the wilderness expedition. Often participants have been diagnosed with depression, anxiety, ADD, ADHD, or oppositional disorder in addition to being chemically dependent.

The program recognizes that addiction affects the entire family, so families are considered integral to the process of recovery. Counselors communicate with family on a regular basis about the progress of their child. In addition, families are required to participate in a four-and-a-half-day family therapy experience. This is called family week, and these sessions are offered once a month. Families are educated about AA, Al-Anon, and the disease of addiction. Then, family and multifamily group therapy occurs. Families are then educated about follow-up and are given suggestions for integrating their loved one back into their family upon his/her return.

Staff-to-participant ratios are maintained at one staff for every five participants. All of the clinical staff possess appropriate degrees in mental health and are certified addictions counselors. Interaction between participants and counselors is frequent. A typical schedule for participants is posted on the program website, which provides concrete information about treatment.

The Wilderness Treatment Center is accredited by AEE and is a member of NATSAP.

The daily cost of this program is approximately $320, making the cost of the 60-day program $19,200. There is also a $300 fee for clothing. Because this is a freestanding treatment center, some insurance reimbursement may be possible. This program has received media exposure, including a feature on NBC Nightly News.

Website: www.wildernesstreatmentcenter.com ▪ **Phone:** 406-854-2832

Other Options

The programs discussed in this chapter represent three categories of wilderness therapy program types available today. There are many other kinds of wilderness programs that cater to specific groups or populations, but they tend to be therapeutic and not therapy-based in their emphases. By this we mean that although the programs might be designed to facilitate growth, they are not providing therapy that is based on individual assessment and treatment planning. Due to our focus on wilderness therapy in this book, we only briefly mention programs that are affiliated with primary or secondary schools, specific programs for health-related problems, and enrichment programs, including leadership and university programs. Our goal is to provide some information about these program offerings, so the reader can further distinguish such wilderness programs from wilderness therapy programs.

One of the most prominent school-based programs is Project Adventure (PA). This program was founded in 1971 by Jerry Pieh, the son of the founder of the Minnesota Outward Bound School. Coming from this background, it was natural to bring some of the therapeutic lessons of the outdoor environment, which are so central to Outward Bound and to PA (Schoel, Prouty, & Radcliffe, 1988). School-based programs are often preventative in nature, attempting to work with children and youth by enhancing their physical and emotional skills. Some programs offer experiences that occur out of the classroom, like ropes courses, while others incorporate more extended outdoor experiences like hiking and camping.

Health-related outdoor programs have become more popular in recent years. These offerings involve taking people with physical illnesses, challenges, or disabilities, and encouraging them to push themselves and experience the wilderness environment with people who share similar challenges or physical issues. These types of programs are intended to provide support and foster an enhanced sense of power and control in participants. Examples of these types of programs include those that offer special trips for hearing impaired or deaf clients (www.outwardbound.org) or adaptive skiing programs, such as the Breckenridge Outdoor Education Center (www.boec.org).

Enrichment programs are different in that they do not purport to be therapeutic in nature. For example, many universities have established programs that incorporate wilderness experiences. Some of these programs are part of academic departments, offering college credit or even academic degrees or certificates, while others are student enrichment programs, offering no credit. Examples of credit-based programs are universities that are affiliates of the Wilderness Education Association (WEA) (www.weainfo.org). Examples of enrichment programs include offerings that sponsor student trips and leadership activities.

Another common use of wilderness-based activities at the university level takes place during orientation programs. These experiences are geared toward facilitating adjustment to leaving home and beginning a more independent life in college.

Now that you've been exposed to a variety of wilderness-based treatment options, Chapter 8 will guide you through a series of questions designed to help you determine whether wilderness therapy is truly the best modality for the adolescent in your life.

References

Anasazi. Retrieved August 2, 2007, from http://www.anasazi.org

Aspen Achievement Academy. Retrieved August 2, 2007, from http://www.aspen-abademy.com

Breckenridge Outdoor Education Center. Retrieved January 5, 2006, from http://boec.org

Camp Woodson. Retrieved August 3 , 2007, from http://www.ncdjjdp.org

Catherine Freer. Retrieved August 4, 2007, from http://cfreer.com

Davis-Berman, J., & Berman, D. (1994). *Wilderness therapy: Foundations, theory & research.* Dubuque, IA: Kendall Hunt.

Eckerd Youth Alternative Programs. Retrieved August 6 , 2007, from http://eckerd.org

Ferguson, G. (1999). *Shouting at the sky: Troubled teens and the promise of the wild.* New York: St. Martin's Press.

Inner Harbour Hospital. Retrieved August 4,, 2007, from http://www.innerharbour.org

Jevertson, J. (2006). Personal communication, September 21, 2006.

Jones, J. (2005). Wilderness therapy and the white hot glare of publicity. *Woodbury Reports*. Retrieved December 5, 2005, from http://www.strugglingteens.com

Monarch Center for Family Healing. Retrieved August 2, 2007, from http://www.monarchfamilyhealing.com.

Mountain Homes Youth Ranch. Retrieved August 4, 2007, from http://www.mountainhomesyouthranch.com

National Outdoor Leadership Schools. Retrieved December 17, 2005, from http://www.nols.org

OMNI Youth Services. Retrieved August 5, 2007, from http://www.omniyouth.org

Outward Bound. Retrieved August 5, 2007, from http://www.outwardbound.org

RedCliff Ascent. Retrieved August 3, 2007, from http://www.redcliffascent.com

Red Top Meadows. Retrieved August 4,, 2007, from http://www.redtopmeadows.org

Santa Fe Mountain Center. Retrieved August 3, 2007, from http://www.sf-mc.com

Schoel, J., Prouty, D., & Radcliffe, P. (1988). *Islands of healing: A guide to adventure-based counseling.* Hamilton, MA: Project Adventure.

Silver, B. (2006). Personal Communication, September 14, 2006.

Soltreks. Retrieved August 2, 2007, from http://www.soltreks.com

SUWS. Retrieved August 3, 2007 from http://www.suws.com

VisionQuest. Retrieved August 1, 2007, from http://www.vq.com

Wilderness Education Association. Retrieved December 15, 2005, from http://www.weainfo.org

Wilderness Treatment Center. Retrieved August 1, 2007, from http://www.wildernessaltschool.com

Wilderness Quest. Retrieved August 1, 2007, from http://www.wildernessquest.com

CHAPTER 8

Choosing a Program

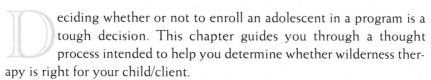

D eciding whether or not to enroll an adolescent in a program is a tough decision. This chapter guides you through a thought process intended to help you determine whether wilderness therapy is right for your child/client.

Our presentation is divided into two sections: "Concerns About the Adolescent" and "Program Concerns." Obviously, all concerns and questions are not covered here. We hope, however, that the questions presented will lay the groundwork for your decision-making process and foster the development of other questions. To make this information easily accessible, we present it in question-and-answer format.

Concerns About the Adolescent

Q: What is your motivation for seeking a wilderness therapy program for your adolescent?

This is the first question you should ask yourself. Did something you saw on TV or read in a magazine pique your interest in this type of program? Have you been referred or encouraged to consider a wilderness program by a physician or therapist? Or did you come across wilderness therapy while doing an Internet search?

No matter how you heard about wilderness therapy, beware of anyone who claims that wilderness therapy is sure to change an adolescent's life or that it will help parents get their old child back. These are the kinds of messages broadcast on daytime television, where teens are portrayed as returning from tough-love programs completely transformed. Wilderness therapy is not a "magic cure."

Q: What kinds of problems and symptoms has your adolescent been experiencing?

As a parent, it can sometimes seem as if your child is the only one putting you through the paces, and that his/her challenging behavior will just get worse with time. Know this: Many seemingly incurable problems are simply a part of adolescence, many of which can resolve by the time an adolescent reaches his/her early twenties. We're not recommending you shouldn't seek treatment for your adolescent; just know that time is often an ally.

Carefully consider whether a wilderness program can help the symptoms and problems experienced by your adolescent. As you research program particulars, you will see that they usually treat adolescents with a variety of problems and symptoms, so don't expect treatment that specializes in just one type of problem. Similarly, most programs publish a list of problems that exclude adolescents from participating (see Chapter 7 for more on this topic).

One of the most common exclusions is active suicidal thinking. However, it is often difficult to assess suicidal thinking and intent, and adolescents can cover this up. If there is any reason to believe that an adolescent is suicidal, carefully consider whether or not to enroll him/her in a wilderness program. Often, the stress of such an unfamiliar environment and the physical and emotional demands of the experience can worsen symptoms. Also, it is more difficult to secure emergency assistance in the wilderness than it is in the community.

In our experience, adolescents struggling with depression, anxiety, issues with anger and authority or ADD/ADHD often do quite well on wilderness therapy trips. Sometimes the combination of physical activity and challenge can help accelerate the process of change. It may also be good for adolescents struggling with depression to become physically active, as exercise may augment the effects of other treatments (Lawlor & Hopker, 2001). If a child has debilitating symptoms of any of the above disorders, it would be wise to rethink wilderness therapy. Participants must be able to cooperate and work as part of a team. Adolescents who cannot do that may put both themselves and other participants at risk, and are detrimental to the group process.

Finally, many wilderness therapy programs say they are quite effective in helping adolescents deal with substance abuse problems. Many teens do use substances, especially those struggling with depression and anxiety, as the substance use is a way to self-medicate. If there is a suspicion that a potential participant is a regular user of any drugs or alcohol, it is essential to hire a professional certified in the drug and alcohol field to assess whether s/he is a user or is dependent. This is a critical distinction: If a teen is chemically dependent, detoxification can be intense and physically dangerous, and should occur in a medical facility—not in the wilderness. The wilderness is an unforgiving environment, and most wilderness programs are not prepared to deal with detoxification. Although it is sometimes difficult to assess drug and alcohol involvement, we cannot stress enough how essential it is to know if the adolescent is using substances prior to participating in a wilderness therapy program. Use of certain drugs has been shown to affect metabolism and the adolescent's tolerance to heat and dehydration. This applies to prescription and over-the-counter medications, as well psychiatric medication.

Q: Have less restrictive treatment options been considered?

In our experience, the least restrictive environment is the best for treating adolescents. As such, we recommend pursuing local options before removing a teen from his/her home and community. Most cities, suburbs, and small towns provide access to community mental health centers. In these facilities, clients are entitled to assessment and counseling services based on their ability to pay. If you have health insurance that includes mental health benefits, this can also be used to help pay for services. With this option, the adolescent attends sessions at the mental health center and lives at home. Private practitioners can also be used for assessment and counseling. Services from a private practitioner are often partially reimbursed by health insurance. Determine if you need preauthorization for mental health services and, if you do, obtain that authorization before beginning services. In all cases, it is important that the adolescent is evaluated and treated by a licensed mental health professional who has at least a master's degree in a mental health discipline like psychology, social work, or counseling. In addition, this person should have special training in working with adolescents.

Remember that outpatient counseling doesn't guarantee resolution anymore than wilderness therapy does. Assessment and counseling take time and commitment (a few months at the least). It is important to know what the goals of the treatment are and how progress will be measured. Usually, an adolescent will want some assurance that the content of his/her therapy sessions is confidential. However, if an adolescent is a minor, the parents or guardians have the legal right to talk to the therapist about the adolescent's progress in therapy. The therapist is also required to inform the parents if the child is suicidal or is a potential risk for harming someone else. If an adolescent gives outpatient counseling an honest try and doesn't make progress, then it makes sense to consider treatment options that are more intensive and restrictive, such as wilderness therapy.

Q: What is the adolescent's assessment of his/her progress in outpatient therapy? And what is his/her opinion regarding participation in wilderness therapy?

Sometimes the relationship between a therapist and client just doesn't work, and another therapist may need to be consulted. Listen to your adolescent's comments about therapy. In order for the therapeutic process to work, there needs to be patient buy in, and the therapist and the client must have a good rapport.

We believe that respecting the adolescent's wishes is especially important when considering wilderness therapy programs, as they require participants not only to leave their home and family for an extended period of time, but to enter an unfamiliar environment that is likely to push them out of their comfort zone. We believe that if an adolescent has an aversion to spending time in the wilderness, s/he should not be forced into a program for "his/her own good," as it might have the opposite effect. In such cases, we recommend exploring other options.

As discussed in Chapters 3 and 5, we believe that an adolescent's right to choose whether or not to participate in a program runs counter to the practice of forcibly escorting participants to wilderness therapy programs. Although reluctant participants often embrace wilderness programs, it is best not to force participation.

Involving an adolescent in the research that goes into looking for a wilderness therapy program helps him/her understand how such programs operate. Ideally, visit a program before enrolling a child. If this is not possible, a potential participant can ask to speak with program personnel and alumni by phone or e-mail.

Q: Will your health insurance cover the cost of a wilderness therapy program?

As discussed in Chapter 7, wilderness therapy programs are expensive, so it's essential to verify health insurance coverage before seriously considering a wilderness therapy program for an adolescent. While many policies offer at least some coverage for residential treatment programs, many wilderness therapy programs are not part of residential treatment programs and so insurance companies must preauthorize this level of care.

Because residential care costs more than many other types of programs, your health insurance company may ask you to prove why a residential program is necessary by providing documentation of failure in less restrictive treatment settings (such as outpatient therapy). Even if this documentation can be presented, authorization and subsequent payment are not guaranteed. For example, if the insurance plan is part of a managed care plan, the program might not be covered if it is not listed as an approved program. Investigating coverage is a difficult, time-consuming task. Don't be misled by wilderness therapy program websites that imply that insurance coverage is possible if not likely, as there's no way of knowing what your plan will cover until you've asked lots of questions.

It's usually even more difficult to obtain insurance coverage for free-standing wilderness therapy programs (programs that are not adjuncts to residential programs). However, some of these programs are covered, especially when fully licensed mental health professionals are on the clinical staff. Again, obtaining coverage is more likely if you are able to document that traditional programs have not been effective for your adolescent.

If there is no health insurance coverage for a wilderness therapy program, there are a few options to consider. Some programs are partially funded by state or county funds and thus are able to provide financial assistance. The majority of these programs, however, are affiliated with the juvenile justice system. Sometimes programs, especially those that are residential in nature, will work with families to secure loans to pay for the treatment. Of course, personal loans may be pursued as well.

While analyzing the financial side of this complex equation, note that many programs are not designed to be completed in a predetermined number of days. Rather, some programs provide a range of days, for example 30–60 days, and state average number of days usually spent in the program. If considering this kind of program, it is important to ask about the range of days and the average stay in the program. This information facilitates the calculation of the maximum fee and the average fee for participation.

Q: Does the family have the time and financial resources to participate in the program?

One of the best elements of most reputable wilderness therapy programs is that they recognize the importance of family support and family therapy to the process of change. Such programs don't place blame on the adolescent, but rather see him/her as part of a family unit. This is an ideal, systems-oriented way to view a troubled adolescent. (For more about the role of the family in therapy, see our discussion of systems theory in Chapter 4.)

Many programs require a family orientation at the beginning of the program. Sometimes this involves meeting for a few hours with the trip participants at the program site. Other programs involve families in an educative process and therapy for a few days before the trip begins. Similarly, at the conclusion of some programs, family members either meet the adolescents on the trail and spend a few days backpacking with them, or they arrive at the program site to attend family sessions and graduation ceremonies.

Follow-up is critical to the success of most programs. Again, this is likely more important in wilderness therapy programs, as it can be difficult to transfer the learning and change that occurs in the woods to real life. Adolescents who became leaders in the woods may need help in duplicating this at home. Also, the highly structured aspect of a wilderness therapy program can hardly be replicated at home. Most good programs require or at least strongly encourage some follow-up group participation by the adolescent and his/her family. This makes it more likely that the family will incorporate the change experienced by their adolescent into the family system and home environment.

Q: Have physical and psychological evaluations been done?

It is critical that an adolescent undergo complete physical and psychological evaluations before participating in a wilderness therapy program. Although many reputable programs offer this service for an additional fee, it is probably a good idea to have an independent evaluation. The psychological evaluation should include testing to assess psychiatric symptoms such as depression, anxiety, and risk of suicide. This evaluation should be performed by a licensed psychologist or a psychiatrist.

Because participation in a wilderness therapy program often involves strenuous physical activity, including carrying a backpack, it is important to assess a potential participant's physical health status. In addition, if a wilderness therapy program's modality involves carrying a pack, ask the program how much weight each participant is expected to carry and how many miles will be hiked every day. Special attention should be paid to adolescents who have asthma and other breathing problems.

Although the previous questions certainly don't cover all of the personal concerns that might be expressed, we hope that by discussing them, we have provided some essential information. We also hope that these questions have prompted the development of others. Next, we turn to questions that relate to the wilderness therapy programs themselves.

Program Concerns

Q: Is the program regulated or accredited? Are the staff and therapists licensed and/or credentialed?

In Chapter 5, we stressed the importance of licensing, accreditation, and regulation in the wilderness therapy business. We strongly believe that consumers of wilderness therapy programs are entitled to the same degree of licensure and regulation of staff and programs that they would receive in a more traditional treatment program. It is critical to determine what the licensure laws are in the state where the program operates. Although state licensure does not guarantee a good program, as we discussed previously, it does imply that the program has been studied, visited, and evaluated by state personnel. It is also probably continuously monitored in order to maintain its licensure. If unsure about the licensure status of a program, ask the administrator and expect a straightforward response.

Accreditation provides yet another quality-control mechanism. Again, accreditation does not imply excellence. The Council on Accreditation and the Association for Experiential Education, however, do use rigorous processes that evaluate programs both on paper and on site. Once accredited, ongoing evaluation is required to maintain accreditation. We support the processes of state regulation and accreditation and suggest that consumers consider programs that have undergone this kind of scrutiny. For more about state regulation and accreditation, refer back to Chapter 5.

Accreditation of a program is not the same as examining the credentials of the individual staff members of programs. We suggest that staff should have the same level of credentialing that they would have in a more traditional program. In addition, staff who administer the wilderness portion of the program should have all of the appropriate outdoor leader and first-aid training that is standard in the field.

Three major organizations in the United States provide outdoor leadership courses and/or credentials: the National Outdoor Leadership School, Outward Bound, and the Wilderness Education Association, with the National Outdoor Leadership School and Outward Bound also conducting courses outside of the United States. These organizations are discussed in Chapter 5. We strongly encourage interested parents and clinicians to contact them directly for additional information.

We also believe that staff should be trained in nonviolent methods of crisis intervention (Berman, Davis-Berman, & Gillen, 1998). If a participant becomes out of control, there are techniques that can be used that do not require force or restraint (e.g., Caraulia & Steiger, 1997). Other techniques focus on deescalating conflict before it gets to the point that intervention is needed. These methods are particularly appropriate when dealing with teenagers who may have trouble with anger management. This is important because some deaths in wilderness therapy programs have occurred when staff was physically restraining participants. Ask if any of the staff have been trained in these nonviolent methods. Also, ask about the program's policies on the use of physical restraint. These policies should be in writing and should be readily available.

We believe that the clinical staff in wilderness therapy programs should have the same level of credentials as those possessed by psychotherapists in more traditional settings (e.g., Davis-Berman & Berman, 1994). That said, this is often difficult to accomplish, as there are not that many therapists who are trained to provide psychotherapy services in wilderness settings. Nevertheless, we think it is important to strive toward this level of professionalism in staffing.

In addition to being more in line with the goals of therapy, staff credentialing is also a legal issue. In order to provide therapy services, the clinical staff must be fully licensed in the state in which the program operates.

Q: How often do participants interact with the clinical staff?

In more traditional residential treatment programs, licensed mental health professionals are typically on site every day, and emergency coverage is provided during the night, giving participants access to a licensed mental health professional 24 hours a day. We believe wilderness therapy programs should try to emulate this model and that a clinician should be in the field at all times with the participants (Davis-Berman & Berman, 1994). This is a difficult and costly thing to do, and we know only of a few programs that routinely follow this model at the present time. If a program does not include therapists in the field at all times, it is important to determine how often a therapist is with the participants and how often individual and group therapy occur. There should be a policy that provides for the needs of participants if more intensive therapy is indicated.

Q: What is the assessment policy of the wilderness therapy program?

Programs should provide direct information about the kinds of diagnoses, symptoms and/or behaviors that would disqualify an adolescent from participating. It is desirable to have these exclusionary criteria, as programs that claim they can work with all diagnoses and conditions are making a promise they can't keep.

Some programs exclude participants who are exhibiting violent behaviors, who are actively suicidal or threatening to others, and who are requiring detoxification for substance addiction. Others often exclude adolescents who are exhibiting psychotic symptoms, such as hallucinations and delusions.

All adolescents should be thoroughly assessed prior to admission to a wilderness therapy program. It might make sense to have this assessment performed locally in the event that program locations require extensive travel. Telephone screening is not acceptable and does not replace a thorough evaluation. If this assessment reveals that a potential participant has any of the previously discussed exclusions, s/he should strongly consider not enrolling in the wilderness program. These types of programs are not equipped or staffed to appropriately deal with detoxification, violence, suicide and psychotic symptoms. A critical part of an assessment could be communication with the adolescent's therapist or physician. Because we are talking about therapy programs, it makes sense for the program to have access to information about prior therapy received by the participant. Prior to admission, families can sign a written release of information giving the therapist permission to release these records. Parents might also sign a release permitting the therapist to verbally communicate with the wilderness therapy program. This communication enhances the child's therapy and helps provide continuity of care.

Q: How are treatment plans developed?

A critical component of effective therapy is a treatment plan, the purpose of which is to set short- and long-term goals and to specify the treatment techniques that will be used to meet these goals. We think that treatment plans are critically important in wilderness therapy programs. These plans should be developed in consultation with the adolescent and with the parents if at all possible. In our wilderness therapy program, treatment plans are developed for each participant. This is usually done in joint meetings with participants and parents as the trip is being planned. It is essential to include the adolescent in this process, allowing her/him to identify goals on which s/he believes s/he should work. These types of treatment planning meetings can actually be quite therapeutic, as they provide an opportunity for teens and parents to talk and to identify problems and issues.

If this planning is done with the entire group of participants, this meeting can serve as the beginning of the process of group therapy. Sometimes this can lower anxiety about the whole wilderness therapy experience, as participants see that other adolescents have some of the same issues or concerns as they do. (For a more detailed discussion of treatment planning, see Davis-Berman and Berman [1994].)

Q: What is the program's policy about psychiatric medication?

If a participant is taking psychiatric medication, it should be addressed with the wilderness therapy program. The administrators need to affirm that they will accept a participant taking a particular psychiatric medication. It is important to determine who will be responsible for administering the psychiatric medication to the participant while s/he is in the wilderness therapy program. An appropriately credentialed staff member should hold, monitor, and administer this medication.

Ask questions about the training of the program staff in psychiatric medication. As we have discussed, some of the deaths that have occurred in wilderness therapy programs may have involved dehydration, perhaps made worse by the effects of psychiatric medication. Program staff should be able to discuss how they compensate for the physical effects of psychiatric medications on dehydration and energy. Do they adjust the program activities if heat becomes an issue? What procedures do they have in place if participants experience medication side effects while in the program? Are there any medications the staff feel that they cannot handle? Finally, does the program have a physician, or a consulting psychiatrist affiliated with it to deal with any issues that might arise related to the medication?

Q: What is the physical safety plan for the program?

It is important that programs have a written physical safety plan, and parents should have the right to review that plan. There should be a physician who can be consulted and direct treatment if a participant becomes ill while in the program. Procedures for dealing with an illness in the wilderness should be clearly presented in writing. How quickly will medical help be made available? Who makes the decision to remove a participant from the trip? How is that decision made?

Each program should have a written evacuation plan to which families should have full and complete access. Where is the nearest medical facility and what is the plan for evacuating a participant to that facility? Importantly, in the case of a medical emergency, how quickly will families be notified? Consumers should not be satisfied with anything less than full disclosure about the program's safety plan, as outdoor settings are more difficult to predict and control than are more traditional settings. Also, it is a good idea to request to see the restraint policy of the program in writing. This policy should clearly detail the types of restraint used in the program and the conditions under which it might be used. Also, documentation of staff training on the correct use of physical restraint should be readily provided. If a program doesn't have such a written policy, cross it off the list.

Q: *What is the program's policy about communication?*
Most wilderness therapy programs forbid participants from bringing cell phones or other communication devices with them on the trip. This is also a fairly standard rule in traditional residential care. The last thing that a program wants to have to deal with is adolescents talking or sending text messages on cell phones. There are, however, circumstances under which a participant might truly need to speak with a parent or other family member while on the trip. The program should be willing to share its policy regarding this type of communication, and if the need is urgent, it should be able to be flexible with this policy. Families should ask for the emergency contact information before the trip begins.

Some wilderness therapy programs encourage participants and family members to communicate by letter. Messages coming from home can then be used as part of the therapy. Other programs are beginning to make use of e-mail and website communication. With this technology, parents are able to go to the website and be updated on the progress of the trip. Sometimes they are even able to view pictures of their child on the trip.

Make sure you know the type of communication devices used by program staff before your child's group takes to the trail. Many programs now have a satellite telephone with them in the wilderness at all times. This allows staff to call for help if an emergency arises. Reliance on the use of cell phones as their emergency phone system is not acceptable, as there are often areas in the wilderness where cell phone service is not available.

Parents should also be concerned about the frequency with which the field staff of the program are in contact with the office staff. There have been situations in the field where staff waited days to inform the office that they were having a medical problem in the field. This lack of communication caused a delay in the provision of medical services.

Q: *What are the daily activities of the program?*
As therapists, we have focused on the mental health aspects of wilderness therapy programs in this book. It is also important, however, to critically examine the more concrete, physical elements of a program. For example, it is important to ask about the physical activities used in the program.

If the program uses outdoor activities such as kayaking, canoeing, climbing, or hiking, it is imperative that the staff have been trained and certified in these technical areas. We have talked about national level leadership credentials already. Although staff don't need this level of training to lead certain outdoor activities, they should have been trained in leading them. Risk management is critical in these activities, and training, although it does not ensure safety, decreases the level of risk.

Additionally, it is important to ask about the pace and requirements of the trip. For example, if participants are hiking, how many miles per day are they expected to hike? Is this expectation adjusted based on weather or on the progress of the group? What happens if one or more of the participants cannot keep the pace of the group? With hiking, it is important to determine how heavy the backpacks are. How does the program determine how much weight will be carried? Are they flexible if a participant cannot carry the required weight? National outdoor training organizations have guidelines for instructors to follow on issues like physical exertion and pack weight. Families should ask if any consequences are applied to participants if they cannot keep up with the physical demands or requirements of the program, and if such consequences exist, determine what they are.

We believe that adequate food and water are essential to the success and safety of any wilderness therapy program, and would not recommend enrolling in a program that feels otherwise. However, there are some boot camp–type programs that do not share this philosophy. Occasionally, a punitively oriented program will withhold food, water, or shelter from a participant if they are not cooperating or are somehow being disruptive to the program. Other programs that are more survivalist in their perspective teach participants to hunt for their own food, and provide participants with only minimal food and water. As with guidelines for the physical aspects of trips, there are guidelines for how much food and water program participants should receive. It is important to see the menu of food that will be available to participants. If the adolescents are cooking, what happens if the food somehow gets ruined or is not edible? Do participants go without eating? Is there access to extra food if it becomes necessary? Is the program able to accommodate special diets?

The issue of water is even more serious than ensuring the participants have adequate food. Again, good trip planning results in adequate supplies of water being available to participants. Programs should provide information about their water supply. What is the plan if for some reason the supply runs short? How do they account for changes in the weather and the subsequent need for more water? If an adolescent takes psychiatric medication, understand that sometimes these medications create a need for increased amounts of water, especially in hot conditions. Program staff should be knowledgeable about the possible side effects of these medications and their impact on the need for hydration.

Summary

Hopefully, the questions and answers presented in this chapter have been informative and have provided essential information about adolescent and program concerns. As you continue to consider a wilderness therapy program for your child or client, additional questions will no doubt be generated based on the particular adolescent and the specific programs in which you are interested.

In closing, we turn to a discussion of fulfilling the promise of wilderness therapy as a viable treatment alternative. Since our first book, we have been intrigued with the promise of this approach. More than a decade later, we remain optimistic about wilderness therapy. Although at times we have been critical of wilderness therapy programs, we are deeply committed to them at the same time. Our only interest is in being an influence to help improve the quality of these types of programs and to raise issues for parents and professionals as they consider these programs for their clients and loved ones.

References

Berman, D., Davis-Berman, J., & Gillen, M. (1998). Behavioral and emotional crisis management in adventure education. *Journal of Experiential Education, 21*(2), 96–101.

Caraulia, A., & Steiger, L. (1997). *Nonviolent crisis intervention: Learning to defuse explosive behavior.* Brookfield, WI: Crisis Prevention Institute Publishing.

Davis-Berman, J., & Berman, D. (1994). *Wilderness therapy: Foundations, theory and research.* Dubuque, IA: Kendall/Hunt.

Lawlor, D., & Hopker, S. (2001). The effectiveness of exercise as an intervention in the management of depression: Systematic review and meta-regression analysis of randomized controlled trials. *British Medical Journal, 322,* 763–767.

CHAPTER 9

Fulfilling the Promise

When we wrote our first book more than 10 years ago, the wilderness therapy field was still young and, in many cases, programs operated according to a set of internally established and often random rules. Today, the field is significantly more mature and the number of wilderness therapy programs striving to integrate with traditional mental health treatment modalities continues to grow—but there's still a way to go. As such, it is our hope that you, the parents and professionals who will largely be determining whether or not the adolescent in your life participates in a wilderness therapy program, have found the information in this book helpful.

We close with two true tales in an effort to drive home the importance of selecting the most appropriate therapy for an individual's particular situation. The first is a cautionary tale that illustrates the problems that can arise when parents do not ask the right questions, take the advice of friends instead of professionals, and let hope silence reason. The second shows how wilderness therapy can provide a breakthrough when other therapies have failed. Names and some of the details have been changed, but the following two stories are based in fact.

When Steve first came to our practice for counseling, he was 14 years old and had been expelled from a private school where he set a fire in the school bathroom. His only mental health treatment before this time was 2 years earlier when he was diagnosed with ADHD and impulsivity. After being seen in counseling for 3 months and taking a standard stimulant medication for his hyperactivity, his grades were good, and there were no further behavioral incidents.

The following year, Steve was again seen when he started receiving failing grades. Over the next year, his grades improved, he was studying regularly, even if just for short periods of time, and there were no behavioral incidents.

At the age of 15 1/2, Steve was caught using marijuana, but said that his use was only occasional. He was also failing in school. Within 2 weeks, he was caught stealing money from a teacher's wallet. He became involved with juvenile court and was put on probation. Subsequent urine drug testing was negative. For restitution, he volunteered at a nursing home and did so well that he was offered a job there. By the end of the school year, he passed his courses, was still working at the nursing home, and had no further incidences of drug use. He was taken off probation.

Steve went off his medication for the summer and got into trouble with the law two more times around the time of his 17th birthday. First, he was caught setting off fireworks and next was caught with rolling papers at school. He admitted to daily use of marijuana when he would leave school during the lunch period. Steve then got into an argument with his father that ended with the two of them fighting on the floor. Steve's mother summoned the police to break them up.

This led to another court appearance. The judge ordered Steve to attend an intensive outpatient program (IOP) for drug use that met three times per week. He also attended some AA meetings. For the next few months, Steve had negative urine drug test results. After Christmas and while still attending the IOP, Steve had two positive urine drug tests, one positive for marijuana and the other for cocaine.

Steve completed the drug program, graduated from high school, continued to work part time, and sporadically attended AA meetings. His remission was short lived. The police found Steve parked in his car on the side of the road. He was sleeping and clearly had been drinking. He also tested positive for cocaine and marijuana.

By this point, his parents were at wit's end. When Steve's father told a colleague about his son's latest escapades, his colleague mentioned a program called Sailing Into the Future that had done wonders for the child of a friend. Steve's parents called Sailing Into the Future, which told them that they specialized in working with at-risk youth. They reported having many successes with adolescents who abused drugs, as well as those who had a history of poor results in counseling, run-ins with the police, conflicts at home, etc.

The parents completed the application process, which included providing a summary of Steve's mental health history, the names and contact information for prior therapists, and information about the medication Steve was taking. Steve talked with the admissions staff and became excited about sailing with nine other teens around the Caribbean for 6 weeks. Before

signing the application and sending in their money, Steve's parents met with
me (Dene), and I recommended a more traditional course of treatment that in-
cluded detoxification followed by a month of inpatient drug treatment. I also
said that if Steve did well with this treatment, he would be ready to embark on
the 6-week wilderness sailing program.

     Steve didn't want to delay his departure and the program recom-
mended that the parents send Steve on its next trip, scheduled to leave port
within the week. The parents signed the application and sent in the $18,000
nonrefundable tuition for the program. All seemed to be going well until, early
in the second week of the trip, the ship docked in port and the participants went
on shore leave. Steve and some of the other participants returned to the ship a
few hours later, obviously high, reporting that they had been smoking mari-
juana that was readily available in the market area of the port. Steve was im-
mediately terminated from the program. No money was refunded. Steve was
back home where tensions were higher than ever. A few months later, Steve
turned 18 and moved out of his parent's home.

     Steve told his parents that he wanted to go to technical school to get
trained as a medical assistant. His parents, hoping for the best, rented him an
apartment in Houston. Before the school year ended, the police wanted Steve for
selling drugs. He returned home, refusing treatment and promising to get sober.
His mother reported that Steve had been shot during a drug deal gone bad but
was recovering from his injuries.

    In their frustration and sense of desperation, Steve's parents jumped
at what sounded like a solution—45 days on a sailing ship in the Caribbean.
They accepted the testimonial about the effectiveness of this program as an
indication of what the program would do for their son. And, when they
called and spoke to the admissions person, she assured them that they had
experience dealing with adolescents with substance-abuse issues. The program saw no need for detox and said they could handle administering
Steve's medication. And while there were no therapists or medical staff on
board, the program assured the parents that the experience was just what
many adolescents like Steve needed to straighten out their lives.

    The parents did not research whether the program was accredited
or even had organizational affiliations with a professional association. They
did not consult an independent educational consultant who specialized in
at-risk youth, and they did not heed the advice of the therapists who had
worked with Steve in the past. And once Steve's parents signed him up, the

wilderness program never contacted his community-based therapists, so there was no transfer of information or coordination of treatment, and his parents had no idea of what personal goals to work on while Steve was in the program.

If wilderness therapy is to be accepted by the mental health community or the general public, it must be seen as part of the continuum of care for troubled youth. Often this continuum is best maintained in the least restrictive environment. Because they are residential in nature, wilderness therapy programs are more restrictive than outpatient programs. They are generally less restrictive, however, than inpatient programs. They also have less intensive therapy services in that there is not the skilled nursing, psychiatric, or mental health care on site. Thus, wilderness therapy programs might best fit this continuum by bridging the gap between intensive community-based programs and inpatient hospitalization.

One of the criteria for moving up the continuum from a less restrictive to a more restrictive, more treatment-intensive program is failure at a lower level. In the case of drug abuse, a person who continues to use drugs while in outpatient counseling might be referred to an IOP that meets for a number of hours, three to five times per week. Or, if a person needs to be in a more restrictive environment, once s/he has stabilized, a less restrictive environment would be appropriate. Taking our drug abuse example, detox in the hospital might have been a better first step for Steve, followed by participation in an IOP. Only after success in these levels of care should Steve have been considered appropriate for a wilderness therapy program.

Now, let's consider a case where a wilderness therapy program turned out to be a good choice. In this case, the participant was referred to a wilderness therapy program as a follow-up method to therapy after discharge from a psychiatric hospital.

Timmy was referred to our wilderness program from the hospital where he was completing an inpatient stay for depression and suicidal thoughts, although he had not tried to harm himself. Timmy grew up living with his mother and his uncle, who was a Vietnam veteran. His biological father had never played a role in his life.

Timmy was very close to his uncle, Henry, who worked in a bakery. Timmy reported having a great life until Uncle Henry was diagnosed with cancer. As the cancer progressed, it took its toll on Uncle Henry who lost weight and his hair, and began to experience debilitating pain. The more the cancer progressed, the more withdrawn and sullen Timmy became. Attempts to help Timmy with outpatient counseling and medication did not alter the course of his worsening depression. When Uncle Henry died, Timmy was so shut down that he was not functioning at school or home. When he began to talk about suicide, he was admitted to the hospital.

When Timmy went into the field with us, he was still largely uncommunicative but denied suicidal thoughts. He rarely spoke to the leaders or other participants. On our first day out of base camp, we took a break for a group activity along a small creek, with steeply sloping banks covered by spring trillium wildflowers. To work on group unity and trust, we conducted a trust walk (an experiential activity that involves one person who is blind-folded holding on to another who becomes that person's silent guide). Timmy was being led by a wilderness leader, Dave, saying that he was afraid of heights but would try to trust Dave as they went up a trail that traversed the flower-covered slope.

They were the last pair to go up the hill. Although Timmy was visibly scared, he opted to continue going slowly up the hill until he made it to the top. Timmy took off his blindfold and joined the rest of the group. Tearful, he was able to tell Dave, and then the group, how proud his uncle would have been of him and how good he felt about this accomplishment. As he looked around at the spring flowers, Timmy noted the beauty of our surroundings, commenting on how much his uncle would like that spot.

Spontaneously, Timmy took off his most prized possession— a St. Christopher medal his uncle had given him —and walked over to the base of a tall tree. He scooped out a handful of dirt and placed the medal in the depression, reverently covering it with dirt. Still tearful he stood and returned to group, saying that Uncle Henry would rest in peace here.

This trust walk served as a catalyst for Timmy, with the help of his therapist, to later gain insight. The exercise did not "cure" his depression, but it enabled him to be more open with his peers, contribute more in group, and join in the daily laughter and conversation of the participants. Timmy continued to write Dear Uncle Henry... in his journal entries, but each one became more of a travelogue of Timmy's activities than the eulogies of his earlier writings. The therapist on the trip was able to use this breakthrough about Uncle Henry as a way to begin addressing Timmy's depression and grief issues. Intensive individual and group therapy on the trip allowed this heal-

*ing to begin. When we last heard about Timmy, he had returned home, was
less depressed and more engaged in the world around him.*

A wilderness therapy program was a good choice for Timmy. He had just been released from a psychiatric unit, so he had been stabilized before the program. Although struggling with a pretty serious depression, he had not been suicidal since leaving the hospital, thus he was not a risk to himself or others on the trip. Although participants can be suicidal and do well in wilderness therapy programs, caution is indicated, as a suicidal person can disrupt the functioning of the entire group. Ideally, a participant resolves suicidal thinking in a more secure setting prior to enrolling in a wilderness therapy program.

For Timmy, the wilderness environment seemed to be the change of place that he needed to accelerate the process of change. Being outdoors and physically active is often very therapeutic for participants who are suffering from depression. Sometimes hiking, paddling, and other activities work against the withdrawal and inactivity often associated with depression. Remember that Timmy was very shut down at the beginning of the trip. It is difficult to maintain this level of withdrawal while on a wilderness trip.

The trust walk served as a catalyst for Timmy, helping him to face his fears and seemed to encourage him to open up and begin to share his feelings.

Of course, these vignettes, like any case histories, cannot be generalized to the outcomes of other wilderness therapy programs. They do, however, point to both the potential benefits and problems that can occur when people enroll in programs. The key is to determine which variables predict good and poor outcomes. By using the information presented in this book, hopefully these variables will become clear as you research programs.

These vignettes illustrate two other key points we would like to reiterate: First, it is important to make sure that the program in which you are interested is equipped to handle the problems of the adolescent. For example, few wilderness therapy programs are designed to deal with substance-addicted individuals. In fact, if detoxification from a substance is needed, being outside of a medical facility can be dangerous. Second, it is important to remember that the wilderness therapy program itself is not necessarily the therapy. Rather, it can be the structure, and a powerful one at that, within which therapy can occur.

Directions for the Future

Wilderness therapy can be an effective and innovative treatment approach for a variety of types of people. We hope that this book has helped you gain insight into the promise that wilderness therapy holds. We also hope and trust that our words have provoked thought about some of the potential downfalls of this approach. Most importantly, we trust that this book might serve as a guide as you explore the possibility of enrolling a loved one or recommending a client enroll in a wilderness program.

Through the years, we have met many wonderful staff, administrators, and researchers from wilderness therapy programs worldwide. These people are energetic, creative, and innovative. They are also extremely devoted to the treatment of those with whom they work. In some ways, wilderness therapy is still a diamond in the rough, waiting to be mined and refined. We hope that our book has helped you as you explore the possibilities and the promise of wilderness therapy.

Jennifer Davis-Berman is an academic and practicing social worker. After earning her MSW at the Ohio State University in 1982 and her Ph.D. from Ohio State in 1985, she joined the faculty at the University of Dayton, where she has been a professor of social work since 1986.

Her interest in wilderness therapy was first sparked by her personal love for the outdoors. In 1985, she and Dene decided to add a wilderness therapy component to their counseling practice (Lifespan Counseling). Since founding the wilderness therapy arm of their business—Wilderness Therapy Program—Jennifer's interest in wilderness therapy programs for youth has only grown. Over the past 20 plus years, she and Dene have led youth into the wilderness and never cease to be amazed by the power of the wilderness as a treatment setting.

Jennifer also has been extensively involved in research and writing in the field of wilderness therapy. She has authored and co-authored numerous journal articles and book chapters, and in 1994 she and Dene co-authored *Wilderness Therapy: Foundations, Theory and Research.* Jennifer and Dene live with their children in Dayton, Ohio.

Dene Berman, Ph.D., is a practicing psychologist and a clinical professor in the School of Professional Psychology at Wright State University. His specialty is working with children and adolescents, which he does through Lifespan Counseling, the counseling practice he and Jennifer launched in the early 1980s. Adding a wilderness therapy component to their practice has allowed Dene to use his expertise in serving youth in alternative settings.

Dene maintains an active interest and passion for wilderness therapy by writing for publications, presenting at national and international conferences, and providing wilderness therapy training to counselors and outdoor leaders. Dene also has served as the chair of the Therapeutic Adventure Professional Group of AEE and has been the president of the Board of Trustees of the Wilderness Education Association.

ASSOCIATION FOR
EXPERIENTIAL EDUCATION (AEE)

 AEE is a nonprofit, member-based, professional organization dedicated to experiential education. AEE provides professional development, skill building, information resources, standards, and best practices.

AEE's vision is to contribute to making a more just and compassionate world by transforming education.

AEE's mission is to develop and promote experiential education. AEE is committed to supporting professional development, theoretical advancement, and the evaluation of experiential education worldwide.

The AEE Board of Directors developed the following Ends Statement to (a) portray how the world will be changed because AEE exists and (b) to provide guidance for association work. The Ends Statement reads:

Members of the Association for Experiential Education will be sought-after and respected professionals for their ability to interweave a philosophy of experiential education through a variety of methodologies.

1. Experiential education is interwoven into many forms of professional practice, including but not limited to: education (K-12, higher education), outdoor adventure education, human service, corporate training.

2. Public policy is implemented that supports the philosophy of experiential education in professional practice.

3. Members have access to an advanced body of knowledge through the development, publication, and dissemination of new information, creative ideas, and ethical professional standards.

4. Members and consumers understand that experiential education occurs through a variety of methodologies.

5. Membership of the association reflects the many fields that utilize the philosophy of experiential education.

WHO AEE MEMBERS ARE

AEE members are students, professionals, and organizations engaged in the diverse application of experiential education in:

education ▪ adaptive programming ▪ recreation ▪ leadership development ▪ physical education ▪ adventure programming ▪ corporate training ▪ environmental education ▪ youth service ▪ mental health ▪ corrections

MEMBERSHIP BENEFITS

Scholarly Journal and Relevant Publications
AEE publishes the peer-reviewed, professional *Journal of Experiential Education* (JEE), a collection of academic research, articles, and reviews; the *Horizon* association newsletter; regional and professional group newsletters and publications; and other materials showcasing experiential education research, articles, reviews, initiatives, techniques, programs, and more. A subscription to the JEE, as well as discounts on AEE publications and educational tools, are included with membership.

Networking and Professional Development
Members enjoy discounted fees for annual and regional conferences and can take advantage of AEE's online member directory.

Industry Standards and Risk Management
AEE works continuously with experts in outdoor and adventure programming to establish safety, efficiency, and general best practices. Organizational members who achieve AEE Accreditation provide evidence that their program meets the highest industry standards.

Leadership Development
AEE members are afforded the opportunity to learn leadership skills through volunteer training and development throughout the association.

Discounts on Events, Goods, and Services
AEE members receive discounts on all AEE-sponsored conferences and events, and on experiential education–related gear, tools, and services from a variety of vendors.

Career Services
The AEE Jobs Clearinghouse offers online job postings for experiential education employment, from internships to directorships. Additionally, AEE conferences offer career workshops, mentoring, résumé postings, and more.

HOW YOU CAN PARTICIPATE

Annual Conferences
Every November, the association convenes an annual conference of more than 900 attendees, with hundreds of workshops, internationally recognized speakers and presenters, and more. Our signature event provides professional development and renewal, skill building, continuing education units, and unsurpassed networking and community-building opportunities.

Regions and Regional Conferences
AEE's eight regions sponsor regional conferences, playdays, seminars, and other activities so members and the local experiential education community can participate and network in smaller, more accessible and intimate settings.

Professional Groups

AEE professional groups represent specific areas of practice and offer opportunities for members to share knowledge and build skills with others who share similar professional interests within experiential education.

Involvement in any of the above activities, at any level, is a great way to become more involved in the association, expand your network, and get the most out of an AEE membership.

JOIN US!

Memberships are available at different levels and benefit structures. See all the details and join online.

www.aee.org